ARCHITECTURE IN PERSPECTIVE 10

A Competitive Exhibition of Architectural Delineation

ROCKPORT
PUBLISHERS

*The American Society of
Architectural Perspectivists*

C o n t e n t s

Acknowledgments

This expanded Tenth Anniversary catalogue of Architecture in Perspective was produced with the assistance and professional skills of the following individuals—Cover Design and Art Direction: Dario Tainer AIA, Chicago; Design, Layout and Production Co-ordination: John Deputy, MetroDesign, Boston; Administration and Organization: Frank Costantino, Boston; Bill Hook, Seattle; Alexandra Lee, Boston; Steve Oles, FAIA, Boston; Tamotsu Yamamoto, Boston; Copywriting and Editing: Gordon Grice, OAA, MRAIC, Toronto; Additional Copywriting: Chris Bruce, Seattle; Jury Evaluations: Chris Bruce, Seattle; David Hoedemaker, FAIA, Seattle; Paul Schell, Seattle. The funding for this catalogue and exhibition is provided in part by each of the selected member artists. ASAP also wishes to acknowledge the generous support of the Otis Elevator Company, a division of United Technologies.

Published by Rockport Publishers
146 Granite Street
Rockport, Massachusetts 01966-1299

ISBN 1-56496-249-0

© 1995 American Society of Architectural Perspectivists (ASAP) and contributing artists

Manufactured in Singapore by Regent Production Services Pte. Ltd.

Foreword

If the truth be told, perspectivists have a wickedly tough row to hoe. They are the servants of servants—unless the client happens to want a pretty picture but is too cheap to hire an architect, in which case they are just servants. So why should the tenth anniversary of the American Society of Architectural Perspectivists be the occasion for anything more than a sympathetic shrug and a condescending nod? Here's why.

In the age of cyberspace, perspectivists may be the last true romantics. And how could it be otherwise? For they alone celebrate in their art that supreme distillation of romance, the vanishing point. Has there ever been an invention of the human mind so irresistibly alluring, so mysteriously seductive, so real yet elusive, in sum so essentially and ineluctably romantic as is the vanishing point? Not the least of its romantic qualities is its name. As anyone who has ever constructed a perspective drawing knows, this passionately imagined, infinitely distant point in space is actually nothing more than the point of convergence for a few straight lines inscribed on a flat surface. But to call it such would deprive it of all its romance.

Let us then salute the one art that finds its origin in the vanishing point; and let us salute also those who, following in the great tradition, today dedicate themselves to the practice of that art. Through their skilfully-rendered representations of architectural visions, they remind us, as we now more than ever need to be reminded, that we are all at heart romantics.

Henry N. Cobb, FAIA

ASAP founders (l to r)
Steve Rich, AIA; Steve Oles, FAIA; Frank Costantino,
at Atlanta's High Museum of Art, May, 1995.

Throughout the ten years of its existence, the American Society of Architectural Perspectivists has published an annual catalogue which documents the year's events—the annual competition, convention, exhibitions and of course, the members' artwork of the jury-selected submissions. That catalogue is titled *Architecture in Perspective,* followed by a numeral; making this book "AIP 10". After five years' existence, ASAP also published a hard-cover retrospective—with the same title (sans numeral) reviewing the work and activities of that initial half-decade. This "Tenth Anniversary Edition" combines those current and retrospective functions for the year ten and our entire first decade in a single volume.

The first decade has been active indeed. The ten years' mounted exhibitions of ASAP artwork currently total more than forty, with the recent successful conclusion of our first European venue in Berlin. Of the ten principal—or initial—venues, three have been on the Pacific coast, four in the heartland (including AIP 7 in Toronto, Canada) with the remaining four on the Atlantic seaboard. Boston has been the host city for the first, fifth and soon to be eleventh convention and principal exhibition of the Society. Currently in the planning stage is a joint ASAP/JARA convention and exhibition in Hawaii, as well as future European venues in Austria and Portugal.

The first decade saw almost five thousand images submitted by members for consideration by ten independent and eminent three-person juries. The ASAP jurors are crucial to the professionalism and fairness which the Society values so highly. Those carefully selected jurors included more than a dozen highly-respected architects, a half-dozen editors, critics and publicists, another eight widely-known artists with a sprinkling of educators, developers and planners as well. It has been consistently the observation of each year's jury that the graphic quality and the level of competition rises substantially with every year's submissions.

That competitiveness is reflected in the generally-held perception that the Hugh Ferriss Memorial Prize is the pre-eminent award of its kind in the world at this time. Over the decade, the Society has developed other awards ("Best in Formal Category", "Best in Sketch Category", and individual juror's awards) which themselves are becoming increasingly meaningful and coveted among perspectivists. The first "Best in Show" has been retroactively elevated to a Ferriss Prize, which was not in existence until the following year. That initial premiated image is the inspired work of Lee Dunnette, AIA, a New York architect/perspectivist who happens to be also the recipient of the most recent Hugh Ferriss Memorial Prize—awarded by this year's jury for the image of Pei's Louvre pyramid which graces the cover of this book.

In addition to images of premiated entries, this book includes a miscellany of deserving submissions from the first ten years of the Society. Many of these works were not jury-selected for the regular exhibitions, but are included herewith as an indication of the depth as well as variety of high-quality work which constitutes those thousands of entries over the decade.

Although the number of ASAP members has remained in the three hundred range through the recent years of its existence, the composition of membership has changed greatly, reflecting the increasing globalization of the Society. Our ties with the Japanese (through the Japanese Architectural Renderers Association) and more recently with the Koreans (through the Korean Architectural Perspectivists Association) have grown impressively, as have our connections with the Australian rendering community. ASAP now has ten international coordinators to service and enhance this worldwide professional symbiosis. ASAP has a consistent history of inclusivity, to which we may now add a current of multi-culturalism. For the first time this year, a majority of the six awards given for the best current work went to other than American artists.

Even the current Executive Board of the Society is culturally diverse, with our next president—Tamotsu Yamamoto—being Japanese by birth. The volunteer five-member Board and paid Executive Director currently manage an approximately one hundred thousand dollar annual budget. With the support of corporations such as United Technologies (Otis Elevator Division), Van Nostrand Reinhold, and several others, the Society is near fiscal equilibrium—with good prospects for future activities, endeavors and growth. We are of course deeply indebted to many members who contribute their time and talent to the cause—particularly all the Presidents Emeriti, and long-standing stalwarts such as Elizabeth Day, the Editor of ASAP's quarterly newsletter, *Convergence.*

A partial list of those supporters of the Society to whom we are deeply indebted must include Wendy Lochner (until recently with Van Nostrand Reinhold), Peter Kowalchuk (Otis Elevator), Thomas Burke (Pomegranate Publishing), Richard Fitzgerald (Boston Society of Architects), Harold Linton (Lawrence Technological University), Elizabeth Muffeney (AIA/San Francisco) and Gwenda Jay (Gwenda Jay Galleries).

The positive results of the sustained and continuing support from within and without the Society over the decade have been recently recognized in the form of a 1995 Institute Honor from the American Institute of Architects. That award is given annually by the AIA to a few individuals and organizations whose distinguished achievements are seen to benefit the architectural profession. In the words of the jury, chaired by this year's Gold Medalist Cesar Pelli: "ASAP has done an admirable and successful job of giving respectability to its profession. Its gain and improvement is the gain of the whole architectural profession." This award, which may be seen on the following pages, seems to define appropriately a decade well spent. As the first-ever graduating class of architectural perspectivists receive their B.F.A. degrees this year from Lawrence Technological University, ASAP looks forward with the confidence and optimism of a young but maturing professional society to the advent of its next decade, and those beyond.

Paul Stevenson Oles, FAIA
ASAP Co-Founder, President Emeritus,
Member-at-Large

B S A

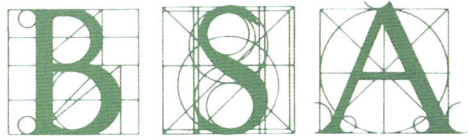

Statement of Nomination

The American Society of Architectural Perspectivists

On a hot summer day in 1984, three Boston-area perspectivists sat around a cafe table lamenting that people who "draw architecture" seldom talk to each other. Steve Oles, Frank Costantino and Steve Rich concluded that a modest exhibition of architectural drawings might stimulate such a dialogue. Accordingly, the "First Annual Architectural Delineation Exhibition" was held for four hours on September 20, 1984 at the Boston Architectural Center.

From that modest beginning, the American Society of Architectural Perspectivists (ASAP) was officially founded in 1986. Since then, the Society has sponsored and mounted nine annual juried exhibitions called *Architecture in Perspective,* which have been shown in over forty venues nationwide--including every AIA national convention since 1987. The three dozen professionals who constituted those nine ASAP juries are pre-eminent in the fields of design education, criticism and art, as well as illustration and architecture. Twelve of those thirty-six jurors are Fellows of the AIA.

Although the Society was originally organized to serve only a national constituency of perspectivists (in affiliation with similar organizations abroad, such as Britain's SAI and Japan's JARA), an unexpectedly high level of international interest has prompted the globalization of ASAP. A third of this year's fifty-four exhibition winners were submitted by foreign members from Austria to Australia. The Society's highest recognition of graphic excellence--the Hugh Ferriss Memorial Prize--has become the most visible and coveted award of its kind among the world-wide community of practicing architectural perspectivists.

The effects of the exhibitions, awards, publications and seminars sponsored by the Society in its first decade have been manifold. ASAP's stated purpose of "raising the standards of design drawing" is certainly being accomplished, as evidenced by the nine *Architecture in Perspective* catalogues. The creation of nothing less than a new design <u>profession</u> has been accelerated by ASAP, leading to the recent establishment--by Lawrence Technological University--of the world's first degree-granting curriculum in Architectural Illustration.

This new profession is complementary to and supportive of the larger one of architecture. In 1940, Hugh Ferriss wrote "Rendering is a means toward an end; that end is architecture". ASAP is providing a positive impetus to higher standards of achievement in the <u>representation</u> of architecture, and consequently to higher standards of architecture itself.

The Boston Society of Architects wishes to recognize the important contribution by this group of valued collaborators through our nomination of the American Society of Architectural Perspectivists for the 1995 Institute Honors Program.

Board of Directors
Boston Society of Architects

The Boston Society of Architects
52 Broad Street
Boston, Massachusetts 02109-4301

617-951-1433
800-662-1235 (in Mass.)
fax: 617-951-0845

A Chapter of
the American Institute
of Architects

THE AMERICAN INSTITUTE OF ARCHITECTS
IS PLEASED TO CONFER THIS

1995 INSTITUTE HONOR

UPON

THE AMERICAN SOCIETY OF ARCHITECTURAL PERSPECTIVISTS

THROUGH ITS ANNUAL JURIED EXHIBITIONS,
AWARDS, PUBLICATIONS, AND SEMINARS,
THIS INTERNATIONAL ORGANIZATION OF ARCHITECTURAL ILLUSTRATORS
HAS RAISED THE STANDARDS OF ARCHITECTURAL DESIGN GRAPHICS
AND ACQUAINTED THE PUBLIC WITH THEIR IMPORTANCE.

Chester A. Widom

President

May 1995

Architecture In Perspective is a traveling exhibition and, unlike its subject matter, highly mobile. The fifty-two drawing and paintings shown on the following pages will, from their public debut in Seattle, cover many thousands of miles, visiting a half-dozen or so venues before being returned to their owners and passing the baton to AIP 11.

Because the exhibition is selected, assembled and circulated in a relatively short time (18 to 20 months start to finish), the work is always current, but the schedule is, necessarily, flexible. Readers of this catalogue are encouraged to contact ASAP's head office in Boston for a current list of exhibit venues. ASAP also welcomes inquiries from groups or individuals wishing to sponsor a showing of *Architecture In Perspective* in their area. As handsome as this catalogue may be, the work can best be appreciated in its original form.

In addition to its public and private gallery showings in the US, Canada and abroad, *Architecture In Perspective* has appeared at every AIA annual convention since 1987.

Opening venues of previous *Architecture In Perspective* exhibitions:

AIP 1: The Boston Architectural Center
AIP 2: LTV Pavilion, Dallas
AIP 3: Pacific Design Center, Los Angeles
AIP 4: The Art Institute of Chicago
AIP 5: World Trade Center, Boston
AIP 6: The Urban Center, New York
AIP 7: The Design Exchange , Toronto
AIP 8: The Chicago Architecture Foundation
AIP 9: The Contract Design Center, San Francisco

Earle Duff—1962 World's Fair, Seattle, Washington
John Graham Associates / DLR Group

When Earle Duff unveiled a rendering complete with
spotlights coursing over the structure at night, hearts
were lost; the spectators emitted low whistles and the
title "Space Needle" was coined. Image courtesy of
the Architects.
Gouache, 44x39

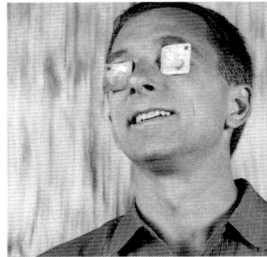

Chris Bruce

David Hoedemaker

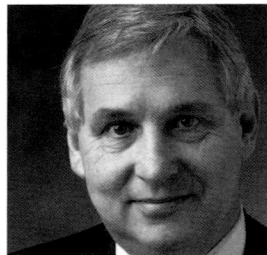

Paul Schell

After viewing over 550 slides from around the world, it is tempting to conclude that the job of the architectural perspectivist is to make good architecture look exciting and to obscure bad architecture enough so it seems tolerable. This is after all, a client-driven art of persuasion. And yet, "persuasiveness" is a more complex issue than it may first seem.

I would argue that all art is essentially persuasive. The first criterion of good art is that it coerces the viewer's attention, and then, that it convinces us the time is well spent in open-ended contemplation. In fine art, the essential focus of persuasion is that the maker is someone with unique and worthwhile insights into life in general and the field of art in particular, and that what is produced is the direct mystical vehicle of those insights.

The architectural perspectivist has a persuasive purpose that is less self-referential. This is a professional field of endeavor with clear standards, a relatively anonymous art form that is made use of by a variety of individuals and groups—by architects to convince developers of a particular design, by developers to convince communities of the wisdom of development, and by organizations to convince funders of the community good of a given project. The highest praise an architectural rendering normally receives is, "Oh, that would be fabulous!" meaning, the proposed building is seen as a benefit to the site and the community. At its most basic level the successful drawing, painting or CAD print needs to sum up "fabulous" and evoke all the positive attributes a building was ever capable of.

After you see a few hundred of these works, you begin to sense various client-types behind the scenes, a code set down precisely by the way the work is rendered. You know, different styles for different occasions. For instance, office towers are often portrayed in a kind of "Superman perspective" (from way below or high above)—the building appears faster than a speeding bullet and capable of leaping (other) buildings at a single bound. A municipal development, whether it is a new school or a complex of multi-use buildings, is normally presented in "seamless restraint" in relation to its context, placed just below the horizon line, so the new development fits into the wonderful, preexisting fabric of the wonderful, preexisting municipality. Another genre seems entirely reserved for proposals for Olympic Games, where new stadia shimmer in the dark and where old airbrushes go to die.

And then, every once in a while, you come across a drawing or painting that transcends the transparent needs of a client, and simply argues for the joy of looking, and for the great pleasure of previsualizing architecture. Such work reminds us of the human fascination with illusion, that after 600 years of perspective, we remain entranced by our own perceptual capacity to see depth in

Richard Artschwager—High-Rise Apartment
Image courtesy of Smith College Museum of Art

a flat surface. It also speaks to the presence of the artist over the obvious requirements of the job. The client gets more than he or she bargained for and the rest of us get one more great drawing. This publication and competition represent an attempt to acknowledge work that stands out with the high points of the past, while simultaneously setting benchmarks for the future.

Writing about Brunelleschi several years ago, historian Giulio Carlo Argan suggested that perspective "is not a constant law but a moment in the history of space." He thus positions early breakthroughs in perspective within a history of Western art that includes Impressionism, Cubism, and Surrealism. In the context of our discussion, his writing suggests the value of an exchange between art and architecture, for these are two areas particularly devoted to exploring the aesthetic space engaged in by human beings. Would that more designing architects spend more time doodling around with perspective from this point of view, at least as a therapeutic respite from dealing with the flat needs of program, plan and cost per square foot. Maybe take a pencil and drawing pad on that next flight to Singapore along with the contract documents and lap-top—just for fun! Look what it did for Frank Gehry. After all, perspective implies awareness brought to the service of ideas, "the interrelation in which parts of a subject are mentally viewed," as well as a scientific means of portraying distance.

Perspective begins by determining a place to begin from, a particular point of view, and this is as meaningful a symbolic decision as it is a mechanical one. Another Renaissance historian, Norris Kelly Smith, recently wrote about perspective in these terms: "the crux of the matter lies not in vanishing point but in standpoint." That is, a place from which to take a stand on something that matters, both to the artist and the client/patron. Of course, both Norris and Argan were writing about fine art, about the freedom to reinvent how we see the world around us. This is not our exact purpose here, but we may gain some, uh, perspective by considering where fine art and perspective intersect and where they separate.

Interestingly enough, one of the primary differences between great architectural perspective and great fine art images of architecture is that the artists generally respond to preexisting realities, where the architectural perspectivist creates full-blown fictions. You could say that perspectivists act within a common desire to see the most positive aspects of what is not yet built, while painters attempt to uncover the hidden mysteries of what has not yet been felt. Fine art offers idiosyncratic interpretations of the outside world, personalized sites that evoke a variety of often conflicting issues, emotions, and philosophical points of view.

Edward Hopper's paintings of the 1930s and 40s are well-known examples. His buildings feel like nothing less than the containers of loss, stoically awaiting a redemption that may arrive too late (a particularly hollow redemption). He interiorizes these external locales entirely, which is why his paintings so often exist in transitional times of day: the cold light of morning, the creeping twilight of dusk, or the isolating darkness of night. Light is used invasively, to expose that which seems more at home in the shadows that are always nearby. His technique is on the stiff side, determinedly laying out forms that brace against an uncertain outer world.

Richard Artschwager's paintings of suburban homes and high-rise apartments from the mid-1960s isolate the architectural image in much the same way a perspectivist would. The original source of these images derived from realtors' advertisements, and they are portrayed with a banal, dirty-colored pointillism that conveys a ghostly ambivalence. His work presents not so much architecture as object, but as a veil of transparent questions about the cloistered conformity of life within.

Ed Ruscha's work from the same time period begs some of the same questions with a more overt irony as well as a comic theatricality that plays off his fascination with the pervasive influence of popular culture. His famous Standard Station paintings are graphic beacons of antiseptic dependability set in the blackness of infinite desert nights. Gas pumps stand as lines of honor guards and the huge sign (and Ruscha's own style) as a tribute to brand-name uniformity, refuge—and attraction. Both Ruscha and Artschwager use images of our built environment to express mixed-messages of pleasure and discomfort, fascination and critique.

In terms of pure technique, the photorealist painters of the 1970s share a rather direct kinship with the aims of perspectivist work. Robert Bechtle's images of neighborhoods in the San Francisco Bay Area and Richard Estes' paintings of Times Square use an intentionally depersonalized photographic style to organize the play of light over the surfaces of buildings and the complex reflections in storefront windows or automobiles. The uncommon stillness of their scenes (often absent of people) produce an overall dispassion that can be as unsettling as it is beautifully rendered. Again, the primary difference between the architectural perspectivist and the photorealist is that their meticulous paintings are based on something that already exists. In that dialogue between photographic image and painting we look for commentary and only find signs advertising gin, coffee or movies; we compare it with our daily experience and we find it looks all too similar; we look for opinions of the artist and find only reflections. What this means is the artist is willing to go to an incredible amount of work to make art that is about nothing but appearances, for no apparent reason.

Perspective, on the other hand, has a very specific reason for being, which is to make people feel good about architecture. It seems significant that in terms of intentionality, the closest parallel between art and architectural perspective may have been the paintings of artists like Charles Sheeler from the 1920s and 30s. Indeed, it is quite remarkable to note how close the fields were in the 20s when we compare Hugh Ferriss' spectacular series of drawings entitled *The Metropolis of Tomorrow* with Joseph Stella's magical bridges, Sheeler's skyscrapers or some of Georgia O'Keefe's city paintings. They all looked at modern architecture with an ecstatic curiosity born of an age that had not yet been confronted with the Depression or the failures of project architecture or the daily reminder of architectural absence we now encounter: homelessness. You get a sense of how times change by reading their titles: Charles Demuth's 1921 painting, *Incense of a New Church*, depicts a scene of great billowing clouds of smoke that weave around factory chimneys. These artists used streaking, mythical light

Charles Sheeler—Skyscrapers
Image courtesy of The Phillips Collection, Washington, D.C.

to showcase the various planes of the American city as something of a living example of what Picasso and Braque had explored in Cubism. Ferriss and his painter-counterparts celebrated architectural forms as dynamic images of harmony, order and even hope, as an outgrowth of American prosperity. This is how we want to see architecture.

It is fair to say that all of us involved in this program love the built environment. Cities and buildings are emotional occasions for us. We want to believe that we are better for having gone to the trouble of adding something to an already dense urban landscape or an increasingly developed outlying area. In other words, we're ready to be convinced. We are a captive audience, co-conspirators in the fiction of what a piece of architecture can be like.

" Happy campers are all alike; every
unhappy camper is unhappy in his own way."
(New Yorker cartoon)

Edward Joseph Ruscha,—Standard Station, Amarillo, Texas, 1963.
Image courtesy of Hood Museum of Art, Dartmouth College, Hanover, NH
Gift of James J. Meeker, Class of 1958, in memory of Lee English.

In such a climate, there exists an opportunity for the artist to teach us something about the process. At least since Delacroix, great art has generally conveyed something of the struggle of its own making. Great architectural perspective gets through process to the subject matter quicker. We see the fully formed product, but not the journey. The finished work is supposed to make things look easy—including, one assumes, the imminent building process itself.

Still, there is a role for a better understanding of the discipline. This is where the sketch can add so much, particularly as an expression of the private exchange between architect and illustrator. I am referring to "sketch" as the true feeling-out of what a building can look like, not as a not-quite-finished final rendering. I mean, what've you got to lose? Do the finished piece the way you think you have to, but in the meantime, let it rip! The sketch is an area that begs for greater representation for several reasons: to show us how ideas evolve, to showcase the sparks whereby the medium is pushed to new heights (it will happen in process, not at resolution), and to convince us that there is something lost in the hands if not the synapses if we give up our pencils for the CAD or indeed, if CAD sketches in its own inimitable way—which is, of course, the real question of the future!

In perhaps the last plastic art form that still insists on real competence, we are often reminded of the utilitarian role of mere likeness. This is the entry level. It's a lot like white people playing the blues—knowing the chords just ain't the whole thing. The best architectural perspective drawings offer evidence of the persuasive value of eloquence. You know these when you see them, and in their search for descriptive insight into the subject they convey something like the clear joy of coming up with a really good idea. In the visual realm, eloquence is equated with what is beautiful—the agency that causes visual pleasure in the beholder. And so, we finally argue for the evolutionary value of beauty. Evolutionary because, as in other areas of human endeavor, the field of architectural perspective ultimately progresses from its glowing successes. Eloquence is effective communication. Beauty is eloquent. Success is beautiful. This is easy to say and effortless to experience, but we know that it is extremely difficult to achieve, which is why this competition is appropriate and awards are in order.

Chris Bruce—Seattle, May 1995

Ten years ago, a bold idea was born at the Boston Architectural Center: Architecture in Perspective. It was the third annual juried exhibit of architectural illustrations to be held in Boston, but the first under the auspices of an infant organization called the American Society of Architectural Perspectivists. From hundreds of drawings submitted from all over the US, the three-man jury selected one drawing to appear on the cover of the show catalogue, one of two designated "Best in Show." The drawing was a stunning mixed-media painted collage by a young architect named Lee Dunnette.

A decade later, much has changed. Lee Dunnette is now a full-time renderer, and has produced an exceptional portfolio of thoughtful and striking architectural images. ASAP is now an international organization whose annual juried Architecture in Perspective exhibition receives entries from all over the world. The top prize, for Best of Show, has been named the Hugh Ferriss Memorial Prize, in honor of this century's most illustrious architect/delineator, and a pewter medal sponsored by the Van Nostrand Reinhold Company of New York City is awarded in Ferriss' honor to the architectural illustrator whose drawing best embodies the spirit of this great man.

One thing has not changed. An independent jury of three professionals, after viewing hundreds of slides of excellent work, concluded that the designation "Best of Show" belongs once again to Lee Dunnette. In the words of jury chairman Chris Bruce, "...every once in a while, you come across a piece that transcends the transparent needs of a client, and simply argues for the joy of looking, and for the great pleasure of understanding architecture."

Lee's award-winning piece shows I. M. Pei's *Pyramid at the Grand Louvre* in sectional perspective tying together the above-ground and below-ground design in a view of this landmark that is impossible to see in real life, and even in drawn form was not easy to achieve. In Lee's own words, "half of the existing building was covered by scaffolding. The old photographs were unusable; and the final viewpoint was largely blocked by the equestrian statue of Henry V."

Once the material was assembled, and using an Autocad base drawing, with photos to fill in detail, "the color rendering was a cinch, and fun to boot. The actual drawing was produced while on vacation in the Adirondacks (mosquitoes, kids and fresh air in an unheated cabin...)."

To summarize the jury's sentiments, chairman Bruce wrote: "Lee Dunette's Louvre drawing...takes literal illusion and combines it with architectural design. He indulges the viewer's complex ability to simultaneously read pictorially and abstractly, and in so doing, makes the most convincing argument for I.M. Pei's pyramids any of us had ever seen. He presents what has been seen as a controversial intrusion into an historic site as a sensible—even wise—necessity, precisely by showing what no diagram, photograph, or rational explanation could ever do. This artist has given us the view no one else can see, and more: through the sheer quality of the drawing, he has convincingly seduced us into believing that we are privy to a delicious mystery uncovered at last."

We congratulate Lee Dunnette on his achievement and on his continued pursuit of excellence in architectural imagery, in the tradition of Hugh Ferriss. We also welcome his work back to the cover of our catalogue, fittingly, on this, our tenth anniversary.

430 East 20th Street, #5B
New York, NY 10009
212.260.4240

Lee Dunnette, AIA

The Pyramid at Le Grand Louvre
Pei Cobb Freed & Partners / Michel Macary Architects

Steve Oles' evocative drawings of Pei's Louvre project are admired by all perspectivists. So why, after 10 years, make another rendering of it? In a word "Paper." Repap Sales Corporation Inc. suggested a visual tour of Pei's Louvre project but found that they needed a section perspective to tie the above and below image together. Lest anyone think drawing an existing building is a piece of cake: half of the existing buildings were covered by scaffolding, and the old photographs were unusable. The entire drawing was modeled in CAD, then redrawn by hand in detail. Although the layout was surprisingly difficult, the color rendering was surprisingly enjoyable.
Airbrush acrylic, 15x30, 1993

Hugh Ferriss Memorial Prize

Formal Category Winner

" In perhaps the last plastic art form that still demands real competence, the most successful architectural perspective pieces remind us of the utilitarian role of likeness and the persuasive value of eloquence."

Juror Chris Bruce's words could not apply any more precisely than to the work of Japanese illustrator Hideo Shirai. Over the course of the past five years since Hideo's drawings first began to appear in Architecture in Perspective, he has established a reputation for producing drawings that combine mind-boggling technical expertise with an unfailing aesthetic sensibility. This year's Formal Category winning drawing is no exception.

In his Sapporo Project drawing, Hideo has deftly handled a subject that would make many illustrators blanch. In one careful drawing, he combines a complex roof structure, a playing field with a soccer game in progress (both shown almost in their entirety) and an audience of several thousand people, cheering, waving, and throwing streamers. With all this going on, the drawing maintains the strength and perfect balance that would be more typical of a sketch.

The jury was particularly impressed with the spatial qualities of the piece: "A feeling of being within," and the compositional legerdemain: "difficult to draw, but the activity balances the structure." Juror David Hoedemaker remarked on the "lights and darks, beautiful handling... colored flags balanced with complementary colors—keeps your eye on the architecture." All agreed that a bold and exciting drawing can convince the viewer of a bold and exciting architectural solution.

We hope that future exhibitions will continue to be graced by such masterful work from one of Japan's most skilful perspectivists.

31.8.213 Honcho
Wako-shi, Saitama-Ken 351.01
Japan
0484.65.1615

Hideo Shirai

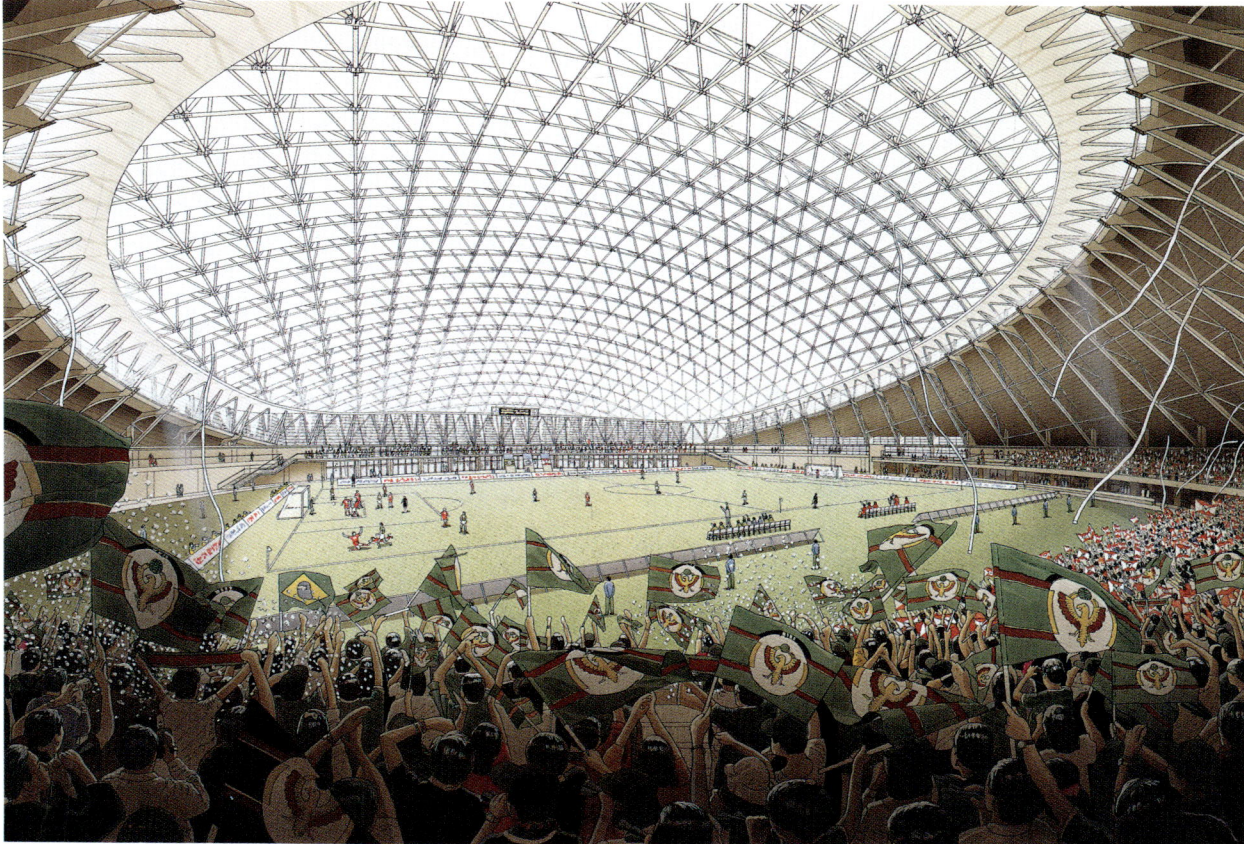

Sapporo Project
Taisei Corporation

This soccer match in an athletic dome is an excited and heated atmosphere created by people waving flags, throwing paper tapes and blowing cheerhorns. The angle of this piece was composed using a computer. The light through the tent-like ceiling shows the contrast between light and darkness in the picture. In order to emphasize the perspective, the distant lines were given a final coating of white paint. This picture won first prize in the Sapporo Community Dome Competition in Japan in 1994.

Mixed media, 16x23, 1994

FORMAL CATEGORY WINNER

This year's jury unanimously agreed that the finest example of architectural illustration in the informal category was a "classic sketch" of the New England Aquarium by ASAP co-founder Paul Stevenson Oles, FAIA. In the words of the jury, the award-winning drawing "blends art, architecture and perspective. It is at the same time inspired and artistic—in between fantastic and real."

Describing the importance of sketching in architecture, jury chairman Chris Bruce writes:

"There is another secret that is delivered only through the medium of the sketch: the private exchange between architect and illustrator. I am referring to sketch as the true feeling-out of visualizing the plan, not as a not-quite-finished final rendering."

In the ten-year history of ASAP, Steve Oles has been one of our profession's most important and influential members. He is not only ASAP's co-founder, but also president emeritus, member-at-large, and a member of the Board of Governors. He is an architect, teacher (Yale, MIT, RISD); a lecturer, Loeb Fellow, and Visiting Scholar at Harvard Graduate School of Design. In addition to these distinctions, his two books on architectural rendering have inspired, even directed, an entire generation of architectural illustrators. It is a great delight to see added to these distinctions: Category Winner, AIP 10.

Interface Architects
One Gateway Center, Suite 501A
Newton, MA 02158
617.527.6790

P a u l   S t e v e n s o n   O l e s ,   F A I A

New England Aquarium
Schwartz / Silver Architects

Speed and drama were the architect's two requirements for this drawing. By photographing a precise, hand-held model in various lighting contexts, the designer (Warren Schwartz FAIA) and the perspectivist quickly agreed on the "iconic" image of the building, and the resulting drawing was based on that slide which was rear-projected onto vellum at 8.5x11. The black and white original was enlarged somewhat by xerox on vellum and retrocolored with watercolor paper underlay. The time of day was assumed to be early morning, highlighting the angular face of the building, and suggesting the dawning of the millennium in Boston.

S K E T C H   C A T E G O R Y   W I N N E R

Wax base pencil with W.C. paper underlay, retrocolor on xerox, 9x12, 1994

The key to the persuasive effectiveness of this picture is the way it reinforces the positive aspects of a city, as opposed to accentuating the sculptural spectacle of an architectural object. It is the renewal of the city which this development is about, not the ego of the architect. This is a developer's project that must work within the preexisting fabric, and in fact, add to it, become a magnet for future development, and fulfill the potential of the place: if the project does not do this it will fail. So, the first job of this rendering is to renew our faith in the value of urban living. But knowing your audience is only half the battle: you have to sit down at the drawing table and make it work. The artist here does this partly by taking advantage of the thrilling conversation between artificial light and sunset, that along with the water become a dialogue between nature and culture which is, after all, at the heart of human endeavor. This is a scenic time of day, but it also has something to do with having completed the normal work day. This is particularly meaningful in a trading city. It is the pleasurable time of day, whether it is about going out or staying home. You even feel as though the weekend might be about to begin: the boats are waiting. The photographic clarity of technique makes us believe all the more in these real-life possibilities. Thus, this is not a simple illustration of what a place looks like, but a promise of what life can be.

7ARTS visuals
Mechtildisstraat 2, Tilburg 5021 CN
Holland
31.13.355341

A l e x a n d e r   B a l l i n g s

Kop van Zuid, projekt I
De Architekten Cie

*Because harbour activities are moving towards the sea,
new building areas are now located in the old docklands
of Rotterdam, the world's largest harbour. Because of
time limits, the photo had to be taken from a nearby
tower at windforce 10.*
Airbrush and color pencil, 23x35, 1994

J U R O R   A W A R D

At first glance, we may think this is nice drawing of a very modest building. We might not know where this city is, but we know it's not Manhattan, Rio de Janeiro, or even Seattle, for that matter. We're not talking about the glitz of light and steel, the melodrama of urbanity or spectacle of site here. This is a case where the artist has reminded us of the reason people started designing buildings like these. They have, of course, fallen out of fashion (we've learned too well from Las Vegas). But here we see how attractive simple lines can be when the architecture is clean and new, when it is made within an appropriate scale, and when it is set in a kind relation to nature, that is, water and bushes.

"At school she learned to draw a map of the valley with the river coloured in blue. It was never blue. Sometimes the Giffre was the colour of bran, sometimes it was grey like a mole, sometimes it was milky, and, and occasionally but very rarely, as rare as the siren for accidents, it was transparent, and you could see every stone on its bed." (John Berger, Once in Europa)

This is a brave drawing. It may not feed the ego of an architect or developer, but it sure makes you feel good about drawing. It may be as close to a classic work of contemporary art as anything here, because it acknowledges the value of the banal. Its great insight is that resonance feeds off restraint, something all too often overlooked in our world. The water is used not as a sparkling mirror that redoubles a striking image of the architecture, but as an unassuming space in the drawing which shows a correspondence to the flat planes in the building. At its essence is a confident dignity that takes things as they are and sees something special in that modest reality.

Jane Grealy & Associates PTY LTD
7.322 Old Cleveland Road
Coorparoo, QLD 4151
Australia
617.394.4333

J a n e   G r e a l y

QUT Business Faculty Building
Peddle Thorp Architects

As preparation for this perspective I took a series of photographs looking across the Brisbane River. I am often asked to paint the usually muddy green colored river as a strong blue. On this particular overcast day, the river looked like beaten grey-green lead. The color was so subtle and beautiful I resolved to carry it throughout the composition. I was very much influenced by the work of Richard Ferrier, whose well controlled, subtly chosen watercolor washes emphasize that color does not always have to be bold to be beautiful.

J U R O R   A W A R D

Gouache, 19x13, 1994

As we have seen in other community-oriented developments, this drawing positions the new building significantly below the horizon line, within the fabric of its neighborhood. And what a lovely horizon it is! The artist has used his considerable skills to celebrate this idyllic, middle class environment, and this is crucial to convincing the local populace that this new construction is about them, not about the architect or builder. But it is not the detail that really makes this drawing effective: it is the nearly pointillist use of texture, an overall technique that announces that not only are we all in this together, but we're equally full of soft, colorful points of light. This is a picture that is guaranteed to ease the concerns of the neighbors—that the new school and an infusion of hundreds of little darlings into this peaceful landscape will do nothing more than knit the community ever more harmoniously together. It is summertime in Canada (a time of year when school is blessedly quiet, by the way), and this is an essential decision by the artist. His decision to set this drawing at mid-day is equally significant because it reinforces the pleasant, unmysterious safety that is at the heart of a suburban inclination. Not only do the children stay within the confines of the school buildings, but the potentially intrusive modern architecture stays unobtrusively within the common texture of its community.

Ronald J. Love Architectural Illustration
3891 Bayridge Avenue
West Vancouver, BC V7V 3J3
Canada
604.922.3033

R o n a l d   J .   L o v e

Glenrosa Jr, Secondary School
Dalla-Lana / Griffin

An aerial view was selected to best show the new school's relationship to the existing surroundings, and to dramatize the view towards the lake and the mountains beyond. To soften the impact of the school, and to show landscape as a "romanticized" environment, the technique of pen line and stipple with overlays of colored pencil was used to give a soft textured appearance to the drawing.

Pen and ink, color pencil, 18x23, 1993

J U R O R   A W A R D

The selected works deserving Awards of Excellence that comprise the following competition category are described as "Formal Category—Formal presentation renderings, drawings, and paintings." In this context, "Formal" maybe taken to mean: more dimensionally accurate, graphically descriptive, and, across a wide range of representation, somewhat realistic. Such work, utilized for the predictive purposes of demonstrating new architectural projects in an environment, must incorporate the scale and proportions, materials, colors, and details inherent in the architect's design. The challenge for each illustrator is to communicate that information visually and interpret it through effective use of perspective and media in a reasonably realistic fashion.

The stylistic variables unique to these images, as compared to those in the Sketch Category, give evidence of a creative, continued exploration of possibilities with the perspectivists' tools of the profession—media, composition, light, space. Perhaps most importantly, these styles of work reflect the artist's own training, artistic capabilities, and aesthetic response to a given design. Such personal preferences, together with other influences, lead to the development of a "signature" style of drawing, quite recognizable in the work of veteran illustrators.

Such refined skills demonstrate the richness of realistic imagery attainable in the interactive process between illustrator and client. The Formal Category winners chosen by this year's jury attest to the increased standards of excellence that are the watermark of ASAP members.

Award of Distinction
This year, for the first time, the jury selected a separate category of drawings which they felt merited special consideration. Those works have been designated on the following pages with the Award of Distinction.

Kantstr 142
Berlin 10623
Germany
049.30.312.1306

Archimation

Friedrichstadt Passage
O.M. Ungers / Tishman Speyer Properties

To accurately analyze this large inner-city block of commercial, office, and apartment spaces, a highly detailed three-dimensional computer model was constructed. The model was used to create a number of exterior and interior studies using different materials and lighting situations. This process greatly aided the architect and developer to better understand various design options and thus improve the final appearance of the building.

Computer, Softimage software on Silicon Graphics Indigo, 18x24, 1994

AWARD OF DISTINCTION

14342 Sunrise Drive NE
Bainbridge Island, WA 98110
206.780.9406

M i c h a e l   B u r r o u g h s

Xu Jia Hui
Callison Architecture

I was searching for a powerful and compelling image to illustrate this building for a design competition. An evening view with the sun just setting and the lights turned on is rich in aesthetic possibilities. We won the competition and the building is currently under construction in Shanghai, China.

Mixed, 29x19, 1994

A W A R D   O F   D I S T I N C T I O N

Rua Do Alto Da Milha, 50
Sao Joao Do Estoril 2765
Portugal
351.1.4671010

A n g e l o   D e C a s t r o

Spree Forum
Jan & Josef Paul Kleihues / Hanseatica, GmbH

Spree Forum service centers will be constructed in one of the best locations, featuring an abundance of light and fresh air alongside the Spree River in Berlin. Built on a computer to assist in the choice of views, the final drawing was executed in ink line and airbrush on Schoeller paper. Photographs of the site helped achieve accuracy in the creation of the surrounding areas. Metallic colors were intentionally employed to provide the proposed building with a technical appearance.
Airbrush, 10x16, 1994

A W A R D   O F   D I S T I N C T I O N

1162 Charm Acres Place
Pacific Palisades, CA 90272
310.573.1155

Douglas E. Jamieson

San Francisco Civic Center Competition
Skidmore, Owings & Merrill, San Francisco

AWARD OF DISTINCTION   *Watercolor over pencil, 24x36, 1994*

1000 Huizen
Lange Geer 44
Delft 2611 PW
Holland
3115.133382

Willem van den Hoed

Shopping Mall
MBO Royters Vastgoed

Facing a large square in Liege, which before our visual modifications was filled with cars, situated in between two existing buildings, the entrance of the shopping mall was projected. The entrance had to be superimposed over an existing segment of the right side of the building, approximately 7 meters wide. The appearance of the glass shopping mall was not yet established by the client and was therefore designed while rendering. Due to the hasty character of the project it was not possible to work with a sunny photograph which meant that the color of the sky and the reflections in the windows had to be readjusted in order to improve the atmosphere of the image.

Airbrush and various techniques, 24x36, 1995

AWARD OF DISTINCTION

Lori Brown Consultants Ltd.
410.1639 West 2nd Avenue
Vancouver, BC V6J 1H3
Canada
604.736.7897

L o r i   B r o w n

Al-Buhairat City, Masterplan and Urban Design Summary
Aitken Wreglesworth Architects / Arthur Erickson

This drawing was one of twelve, plus an aerial view done with Robert McIlhargey for a large project in Saudi Arabia. The drawing depicts the Entertainment Complex on a breezy evening. Al-Buhairat City is a fully planned water-oriented resort/residential community under development by the Al-Afandi Establishment on a 400-hectare site fronting on the Red Sea and the Gulf of Salman, just north of Jeddah, Saudi Arabia.

Mixed, 10x15, 1994

A W A R D   O F   E X C E L L E N C E

7 Bonnie Brook Lane
Westport, CT 06880
203.222.8088

Mona Brown

Stamford Court House
Ehrenkrantz & Eckstut Architects

Black Prismacolor on illustration board, 9x15, 1992

F.M. Costantino, Inc.
13B Pauline Street
Winthrop, MA 02152
617.846.4766

Frank M. Costantino

Tsuruhama Rainforest Pavilion
Cambridge Seven & Associates

*To develop the architect's vision of a 180' treetop view of
this unusual exhibit, a panorama of dizzying height, lush
vegetation and upper canopy wildlife was structured over a
free-hand three-point grid. The perspective was incidental to
the more difficult problem of composing the image space
with selected exotic species previously unfamiliar to the
artist. Also consistent with the client's directive, a minimal
indication of architecture appears only with the balconies
and a sliver of dome structure in the upper right. Assisted by
Arthur Dutton and Judy Pradell. Will the world's rainforests
finally exist only in two dimensions…?*

Watercolor, 25x16, 1994

A W A R D   O F   E X C E L L E N C E

Noni Architectural Perspectives
1531 Delmar Avenue
Kissimmee, FL 34744
407.933.5219

E m m u a n u e l   D e G u z m a n

Hollywood Casino
Fugleberg Koch Architects

A W A R D   O F   E X C E L L E N C E

This hotel and casino complex was proposed with the thought of reviving the 1920s architecture in the area, most of which was demolished or burned down through the years. Though the entire project appears to look like separate buildings in an entire city block, it is actually just a series of facades covering a huge single structure for the casino and hotel. This rendering was one of four perspectives viewing the project from different angles. The computer was very helpful in selecting the desired views quickly and generating the perspectives accurately. Black Lumocolor pens were used for the line drawing and markers were used for adding color. Gouache was only used for highlights and for bringing back the sharp details that are usually washed out by markers.

Lumocolor pens and markers, 24x35, 1993

306, 229.11th Avenue SE
Calgary, ALB T2G 0Y1
Canada
403.265.3304

Rafael DeJesus

Alexander Corner
Calgary 100 Centennial Committee

During the oil boom expansions of the 1920s, the buildings depicted were demolished to make way for new large scale developments. This painting, a part of an art exhibition entitled "Sandstone City—History in Art", was presented by the City of Calgary as an official venue during the 1994 centennial celebration commemorating Calgary's 100 year history as a city. History books, catalogues and assistance from the City Archive were valuable reference materials to create this streetscape of a particular area.

Watercolor, 16x20, 1994

AWARD OF EXCELLENCE

Neubau Imaging
1313 Lord Sterling Road, Box 327
Washington Crossing, PA 18977
215.493.4302

Curt Dilger

The City of Eyes

This computer-generated image, produced on UNIX based rendering software, was made at a resolution of 3900x3000 pixels, and incorporates such techniques as 3-D computer modelling, ray tracing, scanning, transparent texture mapping, and 2-D background painting.

Computer generated, 3000x3900 pixels, 1995

Award of Excellence

1800 Pacific Avenue, #108
San Francisco, CA 94109
415.346.6621

JEFFREY MICHAEL GEORGE

Harrah's Jazz Casino
Perez Ernst Farnet, Architects / Harrah's Corporation

For the benefit of the public, the viewpoint was chosen to include many recognizable elements of its New Orleans context, with the Mississippi in the foreground, and the Vieux Carre just out of view to the right. The Mississippi is many things, but never blue; I endeavored to capture the River's distinctive palette of colors.
Pencil and colored pencil, 20x24, 1993

AWARD OF EXCELLENCE

Gorski & Associates, P.C.
6633 Spokane Avenue
Lincolnwood, IL 60646
708.329.1340

G i l b e r t   G o r s k i ,   A I A

Project "S"
Ellerbe Becket, Santa Monica

This image was one of nine we created for the winning team in an international competition for a new stadium/entertainment facility in Tokyo. In this view we believed the dramatic structure was most effectively complemented by a minimal color palette. The building's designer envisions a constantly changing facade at night with images projected upon solid and semi-opaque surfaces.

Color pencil and airbrush, 11x20, 1995

A W A R D   O F   E X C E L L E N C E

630 Walnut Street
Jeffersonville, IN 47130
812.282.9554

JOHN A. HAWKINS, AIA

Paoli, New Office and Chair Plant
Kovert, Hawkins, Armstrong Architects

AWARD OF EXCELLENCE

The two figures visible in the rendering are the project architect, and the contractor. Created and rendered on a Macintosh Quadra, using AutoCAD and Strata StudioPro, with invaluable assistance from Susan Biasiolli AIA.

Computer, 14x30, 1994

707 NK kojimachi Quarters
7.10 Sanbancho
Chiyoda-ku, Tokyo 102
Japan
03.3263.4813

Yoshie Ideno

The Festival Parade Scene in Edo Era
Akira, Tsuchida

This drawing is attempting to bring back a period over 400 years ago for historical depiction and investigation. Urban Environment Laboratory, Inc. contracted this picture. The details (clothing, roofing, walls, stance, position of individuals, etc.) in the drawing which related to this very conservative and traditional period were scrutinized over and over again, causing this drawing to be redone several times and its completion to take over ten months.
Pen and watercolor, 12x29, 1994

AWARD OF EXCELLENCE

Takenaka Corporation
4.13, 3-Chome Kamirenjaku
Mitaka-shi, Tokyo 181
Japan
0422.42.3795

Yoshio Kono

H5 Project
Takenaka Corporation

AWARD OF EXCELLENCE   *Acrylic and watercolor, 14x20, 1994*

13 Quai Du Commerce
Lyon 69009
France
33.78.64.83.59

Philippe Martyniak

Philip Morris
Suter Suter

A WARD OF E XCELLENCE   *Color pencil and pastel, 33x23, 1994*

WAM Architectural Illustration
3518 Genessee, Suite 2
South, Kansas City, MO 64111.3918
816.756.0378

William A. McBride

Multi-purpose Arena Addition
University of Idaho

It was the client's intent to create excitement and support for the proposed addition to a Multi-Purpose Arena. This was achieved by initially defining the basic building volume through a 3-D modeling program, giving the designer multiple views to consider. A line drawing was sketched out based on the chosen view, reviewed and then intensely watercolored to convey the dramatic effect of performance lighting and creating a more intimate environment in an otherwise oversized space.

Watercolor with ink outline, 8x11, 1994

A WARD   OF   E XCELLENCE

223 Indian Road Crescent
Toronto, ONT M6P 2G6
Canada
416.763.1387

Michael B. Morrissey

The Boulevard, Markham Centre Study
Andres Duany & Elizabeth Plater–Zyberk Architects & Town Planners/Norr Partnership Ltd. Toronto

Inspired by Andres Duany and Elizabeth Plater-Zyberk's principles of New Urbanism as a remedy to sprawl and edge city, this drawing belongs to a suite of six watercolours. The painting depicts a Master Plan vision for the Town of Markham, a suburban community north of Toronto. The tree-lined Boulevard is designed to create a walkable, human-scaled, civic experience. Civic Art, as recorded by Hegemann and Peets in their seminal work The American Vitruvius, 1922, was an invaluable resource.

Watercolor, 7x21, 1994

A W A R D   O F   E X C E L L E N C E

Leo A. Daly
8600 Indian Hills Drive
Omaha, NE 68114
402.391.8111

Philip Sampson

Omaha Civic Auditorium
Leo A. Daly

A W A R D   O F   E X C E L L E N C E

Computer modeling, photography and draftsmanship are combined to produce this perspective. The primary intent is to express juxtaposition of a new facade with the old, bringing a 1950s building into the 1990s.
Computer imaging by Steve Wozniak.
Ink and gouache, 18x24, 1994

Schaller Architectural Illustration
2112 Broadway, Suite 407
New York, NY 10023
212.362.5524

Thomas Wells Schaller, AIA

Untitled
Artist

Inspired by the atmospheric photographs by Andreas Feininger of New York City from the 1940s; this piece is a study of informational layers. The intentional laterally static effect created by the choice of a raised one-point perspective forces the viewer to concentrate on the implied depth within the image, and therefore, upon the overlapping elements of substance, atmosphere and the passage of time.

Watercolor, 24x18, 1993

AWARD OF EXCELLENCE

Jane Grealy & Associates
7/322 Old Cleveland Road, Coorparoo
Brisbane, QLD 4151
Australia
617.394.4333

Tracey Shaw

New Brisbane International Terminal Complex
Federal Airports Corporation

A W A R D   O F   E X C E L L E N C E

The 'New Brisbane International Terminal Complex', one of Australia's newest, most modern and advanced airport terminals, is illustrated as a highly detailed cross-sectional perspective with the specific intention of communicating the complicated function of the building. For this large scale project, pen and ink with watercolour technique was used to portray the level of accuracy required by the client.

Pen and ink, watercolor, 39x71, 1993

Caperton-Johnson
14860 Montfort, Suite 200
Dallas, TX 75240
214.991.7082

Thomas G. Sherrill

Mortenson Residence
Caperton-Johnson

Great care was taken in the design of this project to meet the needs of the owner and to preserve the 100-150 year old oaks. Our presentation also needed to reflect the natural beauty of this tightly-knit neighborhood. Photographs and visits to the site provided the reference material which allowed for such a rich and detailed rendering.

Pen and ink on mylar, 24x36, 1992

A WARD OF E XCELLENCE

Rael D. Slutsky & Associates
8 South Michigan Avenue, Suite 310
Chicago, IL 60603
312.580.1995

Rael D. Slutsky, AIA

Orchestra Hall—New Additions
Skidmore, Owings & Merrill

*The renderer was challenged to accurately describe the re-
configured architecture of the performance hall while still
preserving the center-stage as the sole, strong focal point.
The 1-point, axial perspective helps direct the viewer's eye.
Most importantly, the stage itself is rendered brightest, in
brilliant warm light, as the only light source for the hall.
Light spills outward form the stage, rapidly diminishing
in intensity, and obliquely illuminates the gilded prosce-
nium, the ornamented balcony fronts and the detailed
wall and ceiling vaults. Farther reaches of the hall and
most of the audience are left in dramatic darkness.*
Pen and ink, pastel, color pencil, 22x34, 1994

A W A R D   O F   E X C E L L E N C E

Sneary Architectural Illustration
9728 Overhill Road
Kansas City, MO 64134
816.765.7841

R i c h a r d   S n e a r y

Camden New Jersey Sports & Exposition Authority Arena
HOK Sports Facilities Group

This project was developed equally by myself and Susan Lynn. Our objective was to place a large building into its urban setting, focusing the view to the west to include the familiar Philadelphia skyline in the background. To keep focus on the Arena we tried to maintain the strongest contrasts adjacent and near to it, while lowering contrasts as we moved away.

Watercolor, 6x35, 1993

A WARD   OF   E XCELLENCE

Takenaka Corporation
1.26 Higashiyamamoto-machi Chikusa
Nagoya, Aichi 464
Japan
052.781.4474

M a s a n a r i   W a k i t a

TM Project
Takenaka Corporation

This rendering prepared as an entry for a competition, shows the museum standing among mountains in Takayama City, Gifu Prefecture, one of the Japanese scenic resorts. A spread of space is expressed by integrating the local features—mountains, old private houses and traditional festival floats ('dashi')—into the overall image.

Watercolor and airbrush, 30x20, 1994

A W A R D   O F   E X C E L L E N C E

Delineation Graphix
238 Bulwara Road, Ultimo
Sydney, NSW 2007
Australia
61.2.552.3666

Serge Zaleski, ARAIA

Proposed Exhibition Center
John Andrews International

This drawing was a competition entry for a major convention/exhibition Centre. The site is immediately south of the Brisbane CBD and separated from it by the Brisbane River. It was decided to dramatize the development's urban context with a dusk view. The perspective set-up was done on CAD, then transfered to Bainbridge board for completion in tempera/airbrush media.

Tempera, watercolor, airbrush, 24x36, 1992

AWARD OF EXCELLENCE

The 1995 call-for-entry competition poster describing work that would qualify for selection in this category read simply: "Sketch Category—Informal sketches, drawings, and paintings." Despite the unencumbered wording, the interpretation by participating entrants was subjective enough to result in a rather broad spectrum of imagery.

Sketches are generally recognized to be the result of a technique, rapidly applied, that captures the essence of an idea. The chosen works are just as much the jury's interpretation of that definition since the evaluation of certain images justified the recategorization of some entries.

However, what underlies these sketch selections is the instinctive visualization, design skill, and drawing experience distilled (usually within extreme scheduling constraints) into vigorous, gestural, figurative drawings or paintings that impart a confident aesthetic expression. The power of imagery resulting from this process is quite evident, and perhaps linked even more closely to the architect's or designer's conception.

Award of Distinction
As in the previous category, the jury selected a separate group of drawings which they felt merited special consideration. Those works have been designated on the following pages with the Award of Distinction.

FIRM X Ferrier, Hampton, Quevedo, King
1628 Connally Terrace
Arlington, TX 76010
817.469.8605

Richard B. Ferrier, FAIA

Windows & Fragments—Find it Tomorrow, Touch Me Back
R.B. Ferrier, FAIA

In addition to teaching responsibilities at the university, I maintain a small practice with three partners: FIRM X. Conceptual investigation utilizing drawings and models allows us to explore architectonic ideas which inform and influence our architecture. A broad range of theoretical considerations can be addressed in this manner which results in new potential and opportunity with our architectural and design commissions. My "Windows and Fragments" series of watercolour collage drawings consider such issues as the horizontal condition of the ground, layering of images and form in the landscape, hierarchy, memory, precedence, connections and more. Drawing allows us to focus on image, and potential then contributes to our dialog of architectural response. These drawings are not illustrations of our buildings but investigations which become architecture.

AWARD OF DISTINCTION

Watercolor, graphite, photo images, metals, 32x40, 1990

Architectural Illustration
828 Charles Allen Drive NE
Atlanta, GA 30308
404.876.3943

Barbara Worth Ratner, AIA

McDuffie Satellite Center
Lord, Aeck & Sargent, Architects

The McDuffie Satellite Center, Georgia Department of Technical & Adult Education, offers college level courses in various technologies, especially computers. The clean building design, including corridors opened to the surrounding pines with continuous butt-glazing, looked forbiddingly stark when rendered in a tight view on computer. A new viewpoint from the approach drive was chosen to set the building in its inviting context; watercolor was used for its softening qualities. The size of the painting was sufficient to convey a feeling of comfort and humanity without addressing building details and their resolution.
Watercolor, 6x5, 1995

AWARD OF DISTINCTION

Hellmuth, Obata & Kassabaum, Suite 700
6688 N. Central Expwy
Dallas, TX 75206
214.739.6688

Edgardo A. De Lara

KM-17 Housing
Hellmuth Obata & Kassabaum

*KM-17 is a design proposal for high density housing in
Mexico City incorporating amenities such as health club,
tennis courts, etc. within the limited area of the site
located in a fairly mountainous suburb. Computer 3D
models were used to establish the best view to illustrate
how the project was adapted to the site.*
Color pencil, 11x17, 1994

A WARD OF EXCELLENCE

747 Poplar Avenue
Boulder, CO 80304
303.449.3259

S T A N L E Y   D O C T O R

La Parva Ski Resort
Gage Davis Associates

This drawing is part of a series created while thinking about the potential architectural character of a proposed ski area expansion. It is a spontaneous drawing that was part of the design process at the planning level, and as such contains a rich complexity of ideas and possibilities uninhibited by design constraints. A more refined version of this subject was used as a part of the illustrative plan package.

Wax pencil and watercolor, 12x18, 1993

A W A R D   O F   E X C E L L E N C E

Peter Edgeley PTY LTD
30 Queens Road, Suite 17
Melbourne, Victoria 3004
Australia
613.9866.6620

Peter Edgeley, FSAI, RIBA

Bangkok Tower
The BLB Group / David Cole

The tower was perceived as a pure sculptural form. In portraying the germ of this idea, a color pencil study was drawn in the loosest of techniques. As materials and details were still being resolved at this stage, it was decided to avoid the hard edge of computer realism, and the result is an excercise in simple light and shade and the deliberate use of contrasting colors.

Derwent color pencil and gouache, 12x8, 1994

A W A R D   O F   E X C E L L E N C E

Gordon Grice, OAA, MRAIC

Lulu Island Leisure Park
Forrec International

One of a series of design and composition study sketches for a major presentation of a Middle East pleasure park. With these drawings as a base, and with the aid of a vast quantity of architectural and general reference material, Bob McIlhargey and Lori Brown of Vancouver prepared final coloured renderings. One of Bob and Lori's finished renderings, based on another of these sketches appeared in AIP 9.

Fountain pen on vellum, 10x13, 1993

AWARD OF EXCELLENCE

Christopher Grubbs Illustrator
601 Fourth Street, Loft 102
San Francisco, CA 94107
415.243.4394

C h r i s t o p h e r   G r u b b s

Saigon South Master Plan
Skidmore, Owings & Merrill, Chicago

Just what is the Vietnam of the 21st Century supposed to look like? Beyond the large scale planning ideas and architecture a sense of future life had to be expressed: will people only wear Western clothes and drive Mercedes? The people and their situations in these drawings conveyed inevitably some sensitive social and political messages that caused the architects and me some thought. We illustrators are among other things stage directors, set designers. My goal here was to show a much happier and more prosperous Vietnam, a country that maintains its indigenous character as it joins the world community.

AWARD OF EXCELLENCE

Prismacolor on Canon copy of ink on paper original, 5x8, 1994

Sakal & Hood: Architecture & Urban Design
1012 Colley Avenue
Norfolk, VA 23507
804.622.6991

S a l l i e   A .   H o o d

Daley Plaza, Chicago, October 29, 2028
Sakal & Hood Architects

*To complete (in just two months) the Chicago Historical
Society's commission to design and produce a 19-foot-
long vision of Chicago's Loop in the year 2028, we inked
small, then enlarged and colored, and then really
enlarged. This drawing, the first of a triptych, grew from
7x19 to 10x24, and finally to 30x77. Multiple vanishing
points gave us the 230° panorama we needed to trans-
port viewers into the urban space of the future. The foreground crowd smoothed the resulting fish-eye curvature
of Washington Street and at the same time heightened
the future's psychological draw.*

Verithin over copy of pen and ink original, 10x24, 1988

A W A R D   O F   E X C E L L E N C E

Takenaka Corporation
4.9.6 Futamuradai
Toyoake, Aiehi 470.11
Japan
0562.92.0203

N o r i k o   K a m i y a

K-MIX Head Office Studio Project
Takenaka Corporation

This interior perspective for an FM station head office studio project in Shizouka City shows the multi-purpose hall with listeners. As the FM broadcasting station is a base for dispatching music information, a loft overflowing with the atmosphere of a live concert, where you can feel the fevered energetic air of reckless young people, is proposed. A free artistic style of drawing is employed with free-hand lines and watercolor painting on kraft-like paper.
Watercolor, 12x17, 1994

A W A R D   O F   E X C E L L E N C E

Spaceprint, Inc.
632 Beaumont Drive
State College, PA 16801
814.466.3054

P e t e r   M a g y a r

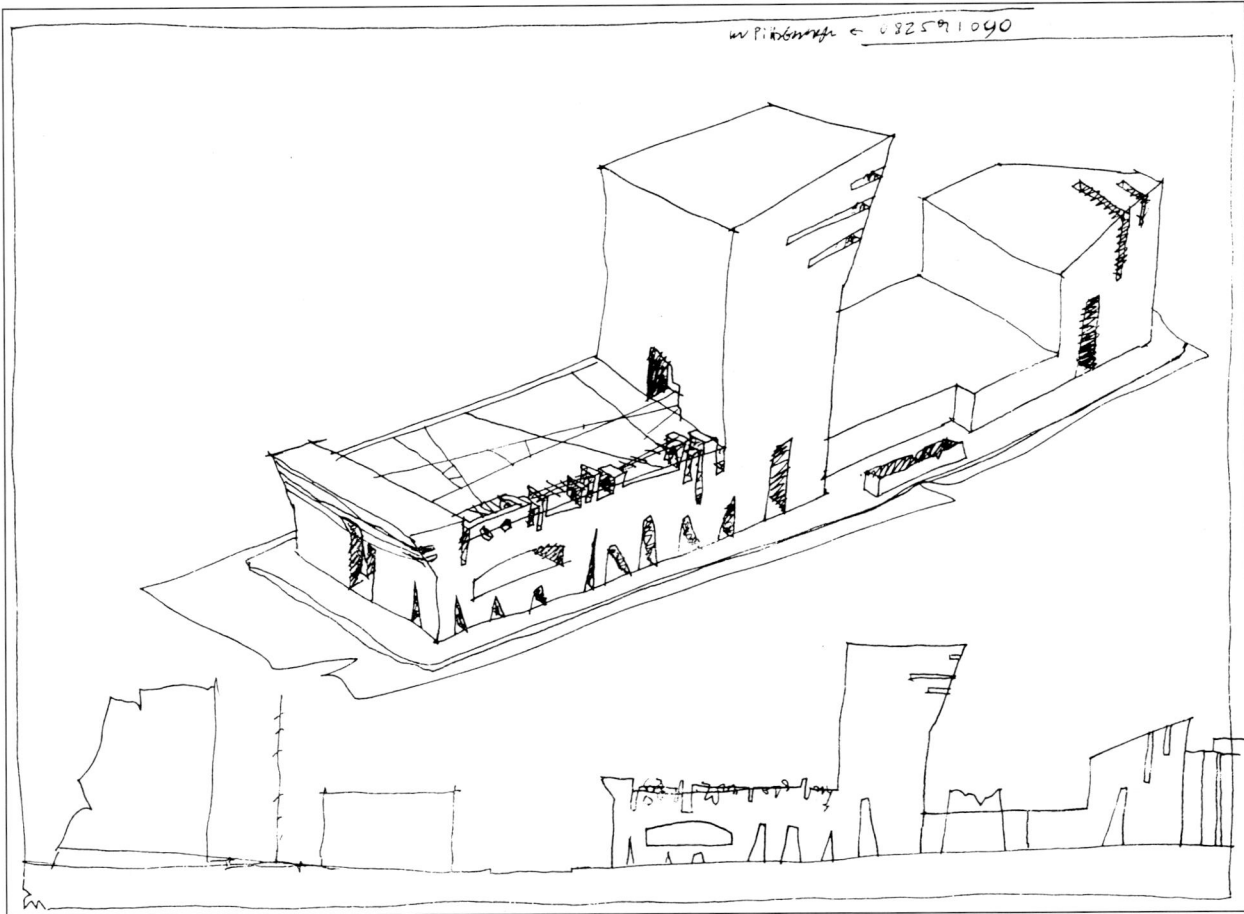

Public Safety Building
L.D. Astorino Architects

The Public Safety Building Complex in Pittsburgh eventually will contain a courthouse (under construction), a highrise office building, parking for 2800 cars and an LRT station. The process of "Image Controlled Idea Development", as means of discovery, progresses from the direction of the unchangeable constraints towards the ocean of free options. As part of our "place response" we set out to recognize, enhance or create visual boundaries. This domain's geometrical determinants were sought after with the "surface drawings" or "Spaceprints". In this way the rationally conceived forms should gain their culturally coded conventions via a subconscious, intuitive manner.

Ink on paper, 8x11, 1995

A W A R D   O F   E X C E L L E N C E

UDA Architects
1133 Penn Avenue
Pittsburgh, PA 15222
412.765.1133

Paul Ostergaard, AIA

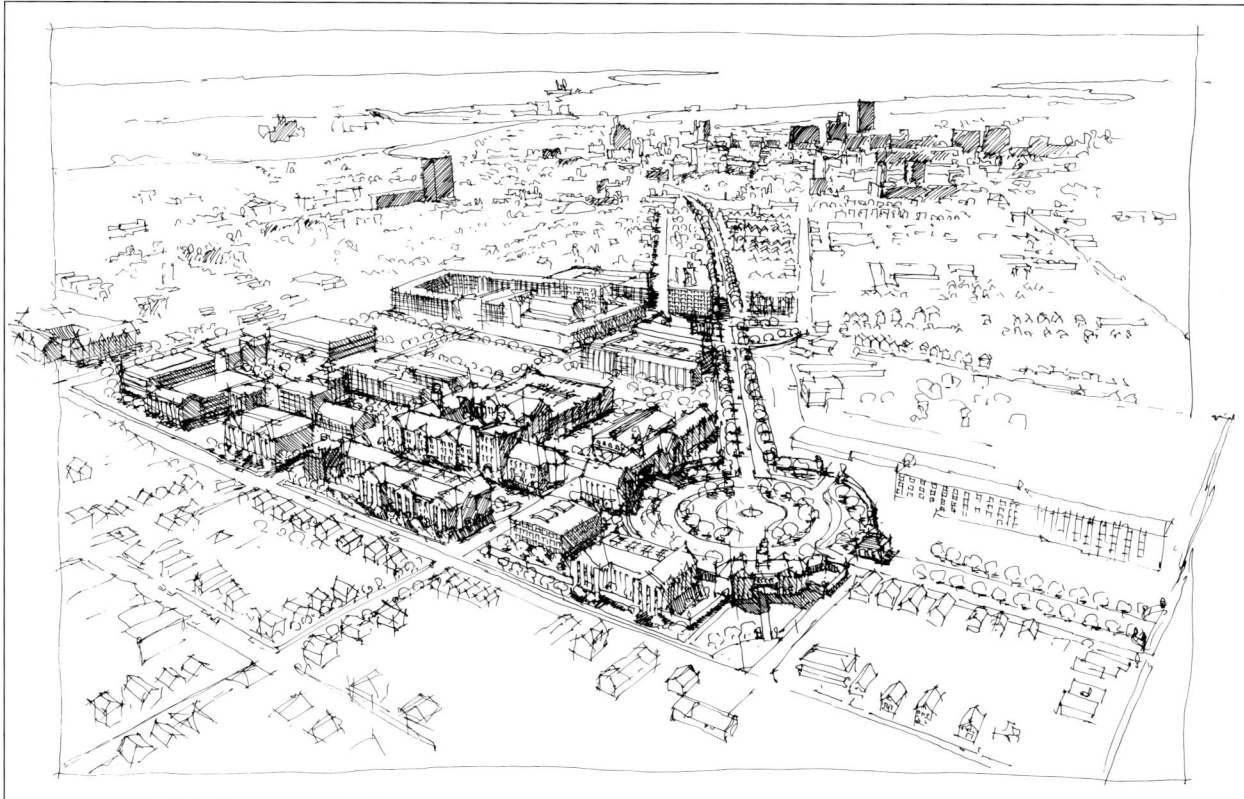

Yale Science Park
Herbert S. Newman & Partners, P.B. Svigals & Associates, UDA Architects

Yale Science Park is a research campus on the site of a 19th century gun factory and near the historic center of New Haven and Yale University. The rapidly sketched aerial view of the proposed campus was drawn with ink on tracing paper over an aerial photograph of the existing factory complex. The drawing shows a new boulevard which uses the right of way of an abandoned railroad line and terminates in a round-about at the science park. A product of a design charrette, the drawing captures the importance of creating a more direct link to the center of New Haven.

Ink line, 9x24, 1988

Award of Excellence

Hellmuth, Obata & Kassabaum
211 North Broadway, Suite 600
St Louis, MO 63102.2733
314.421.2000

S T E P H E N   P A R K E R

Arrabida Mixed-Use Development
Hellmuth, Obata & Kassabaum

The presentation for the Arrabida mixed-use complex involved the exploration of several schemes and views to capture the design concept coupled with the ambience of the locale—a site perched high overlooking the Rio Douro outside of Oporto, Portugal. This painting was one in a series of ten images which were then enlarged to 3'x4' murals and completely covered the conference wall areas, adding to the success of the entire effort, which sold the client.

Watercolor, 11x17, 1994

A W A R D   O F   E X C E L L E N C E

Ringman Design and Illustration
1800 McKinney Avenue
Dallas, TX 75201
214.871.9001

Samuel C. Ringman

St. Angelo Residence
Thomas R. Guerin, Guerin Architecture

In a small watercolor study of a residence to be built on a lake in the countryside near Dallas, the soft, surreal light of dusk was rendered to evoke tranquility of an evening at home. The view across the water of the house nestled in the trees further reinforces the portrayal of this country home as refuge from the city.

Watercolor, 6x9, 1995

AWARD OF EXCELLENCE

Eric Schleef Illustration
7740 Dean Road
Indianapolis, IN 46240
317.595.0016

Eric Schleef

Empire Casino & Resort Lobby
HNTB Corporation

One of a series of drawings used to explain the project to local citizens. Pastel, colored pencil and watercolor were applied to a photocopy of the original pencil drawing. Terry Steadham collaborated on this project.
Mixed media, 10x8, 1994

A W A R D   O F   E X C E L L E N C E

Atelier Szroborz
Merowingerstr. 120
Dusseldorf 40225
Germany
0211.317.96.93

S t a n i s l a w   S z r o b o r z

Kathe Kollwitz Office Building
RKW Architects

The aim of this rendering was to set the proposed building in strong contrast to the adjacent existing classical structures with their bay windows and numerous architectural details. A traditional punched window facade underscores the neutral outward appearance of Käthe-Kollwitz House. A glass tower projecting dramatically out from the facade will emphasize the building's corner location. While the new facade succeeds in creating contrast with the neighboring structures, the body of the building is scaled to match the adjacent building heights. The ground floor is planned for commercial usage and the upper floors for office functions. Residential units are located on the 6th and 7th floors, some of which expand up into glass corner towers in the form of duplex apartments.

Mixed media on canvas, 20x28, 1995

A w a r d   o f   E x c e l l e n c e

NPS und Partner
Ulmenstrasse 40
22299 Hamburg
Germany
49.40.48061848

S e r g e i   E .   T c h o b a n

Elephants House Competition
Nietz, Prasch, Sigl und Partner Architekten BDA

A W A R D   O F   E X C E L L E N C E

One of the perspectives for the competition of the New Architectural proposal conception for the Elephants House in the Dresden Zoological garden.
Prismacolor on paper, 12x16, 1994

Tolon Design
814 Camelia Street
Berkeley, CA 94710
510.528.3007

Canan Tolon

Untitled

AWARD OF EXCELLENCE   *Oil paint on mylar, 12x12, 1995*

Ralph Weaver Delineator
RD 1, Box 141
McVeytown, PA 17051
717.899.6985

R a l p h   W e a v e r

Environmental Education Center

*Pejo Paese, a small agricultural village at the edge of
Italy's Parco Nazionale Stelvio, is the site for this
proposed Environmental Educational Center. The serial
drawings attempt to suggest the spatial sequence a
visitor would experience walking from the Pensione S.
Rocco, through the project then out into the high
pastures and the wilderness of the park.*
Ink, 19x19, 1995

A W A R D   O F   E X C E L L E N C E

4141 Lybyer Avenue
Miami, FL 33133
305.663.8347

Curtis James Woodhouse

South Pointe Development Competition
Arquitectonica with STA/Portofino Group

A WARD OF EXCELLENCE   *Watercolor on xerox, 6x8, 1993*

Each participant in AIP 10 was invited to submit an image or alternate image to appear in the catalogue. While not all participants were able to respond to this request, a large number did. The following pages contain ample evidence of the excellence of the work from which the judges had to choose.

a **Antwis, Donald**
7 Arvon Street
Beachmere, QLD 4510
Australia
074.968645

b **Aoki, Yutaka**
707NK Kojimachi Quaters
7.10 Sanbancho
Chiyod-ku, Tokyo 102
Japan
03.3263.4813

c **Archimation**
Kantstr 142
Berlin 10623
Germany
049.30.312.1306

a

Alan Gilbert & Associates

b

Japan Toter Company

c

Gergan Marg & Partner

a **Asada, Yoshio**
  11.23 Tuchibotoke Kawata
  Yamashina-ku, Kyoto
  Kyoto 607
  Japan
  075.592.0931

b **Baehr, Richard, AIA**
  305 Northern Boulevard
  Great Neck, NY 11021
  516.466.0470

c **Ballings, Alexander**
  7ARTS visuals
  Mechtildisstraat 2
  Tilburg 5021 CN
  Holland
  31.13.355341

c   *Siemens Bau-anlagen*

b   *Berg & Forster / Trinity Realty*

a   *JR South Kusatu Station Development Union*

d **Becker, Robert**
35 South Broadway N7
Irvington, NY 10533
914.591.5906

e **Blanc, Luis**
30 St. Felix Street, #2B
Brooklyn, NY 11217
718.797.1267

f **Brown, Lori**
Lori Brown Consultants Ltd.
410.1639 West 2nd Avenue
Vancouver, BC V6J 1H3
Canada
604.736.7897

e   *Perkins & Will*

f   *Perkins & Company Architects*

d   *Michael Boender*

a **Brown, Mona**
  7 Bonnie Brook Lane
  Westport, CT 06880
  203.222.8088

b **Buccalo, Nicholas Joel**
  The Drawing Studio
  211 Warren Street
  Brooklyn, NY 11201
  718.488.7894

c **Buchanan, Edward**
  5825 Keith Avenue, #4
  Oakland, CA 94618
  510.654.6755

b *NJB Architects / Philip Johnson, Ritchie & Fiore Architects*

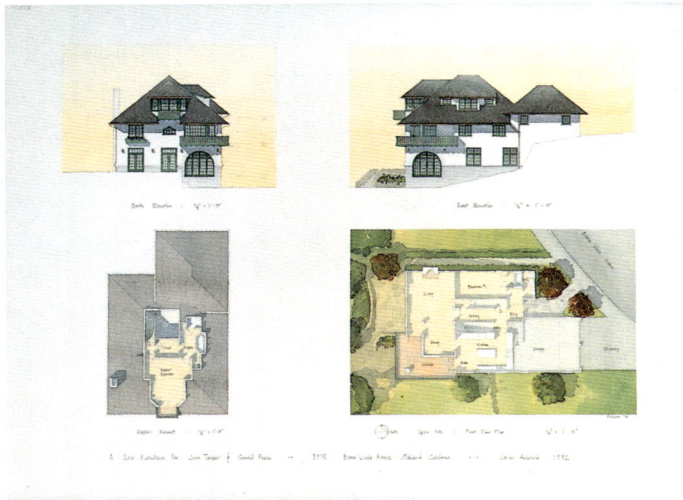

c *Jarvis Architects*

a *Conklin Rossant*

d **Burroughs, Michael**
14342 Sunrise Drive NE
Bainbridge Island, WA 98110
206.780.9406

e **Cermak, Dianne, S.P.**
34 Glendoon Road
Needham, MA 02192
617.455.6334

f **Chinen, Makoto**
203 Diapalace
Yagotoomoteyam 2.401
Omoteyama Tenpa
Nagoya, Aichi 468
Japan
052.834.7033

d

Callison Architecture

f

Kawakam Architect Office Company

e

a **Costantino, Frank M.**
   F.M. Costantino, Inc.
   13B Pauline Street
   Winthrop, MA 02152
   617.846.4766

b **Day, Elizabeth Ann**
   1218 Baylor Street, #204
   Austin, TX 78703
   512.469.6011

c **DeCastro, Angelo**
   Rua Do Alto Da Milha, 50
   Sao Joao Do Estoril 2765
   Portugal
   351.1.4671010

c

Friederich + Partner Architects

b

Burgess & Niple

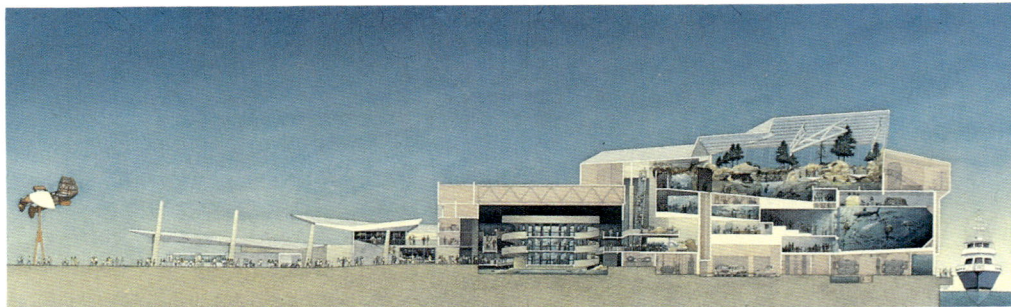

a

Schwartz / Silver Associates

d **DeGuzman, Emmanuel**
Noni Architectural Perspectives
1531 Delmar Avenue
Kissimmee, FL 34744
407.933.5219

e **DeJesus, Rafael**
306, 229.11th Avenue SE
Calgary, ALB T2G 0Y1
Canada
403.265.3304

f **De Lara, Edgardo, A.**
Hellmuth, Obata & Kassabaum
Suite 700
6688 N. Central Expwy
Dallas, TX 75206
214.739.6688

e

LeBlond Partnership

d

Fugleberg Koch Architects

f

Hellmuth Obata & Kassabaum

a **Dilger, Curt**
Neubau Imaging
1313 Lord Sterling Road
Box 327
Washington Crossing, PA 18977
215.493.4302

b **DiVito, Kenneth**
4347 Devonshire Drive
Troy, MI 48098
313.952.5155

c **Doctor, Stanley**
747 Poplar Avenue
Boulder, CO 80304
303.449.3259

b

a

Neubau Imaging

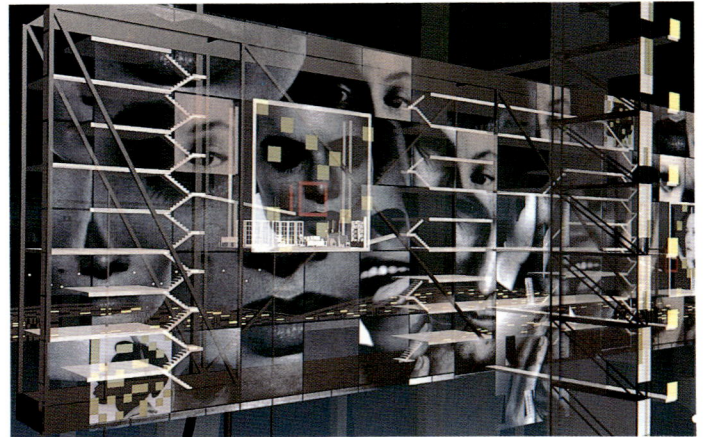

c

Zehren Associates

d **Dunnette, Lee, AIA**
430 East 20th Street, #5B
New York, NY 10009
212.260.4240

e **Earl, James**
17 Parkview Drive
Hingham, MA 02043
617.749.7982

f **Edgeley, Peter, FSAI, RIBA**
Peter Edgeley PTY LTD
30 Queens Road, Suite 17
Melbourne, Victoria 3004
Australia
613.9866.6620

d

Pei Cobb Freed & Partners

e

f

Australian Construction Services

a **Evans, Bill**
714 1st Avenue West
Seattle, WA 98119
206.282.8785

b **Ferrier, Richard, FAIA**
FIRM X Ferrier, Hampton
Quevedo, King
1628 Connally Terrace
Arlington, TX 76010
817.469.8605

c **Fleming, Dudley**
Rockwood Sumner Grant
136 1/2 South Main Street
Studio 1
Bowling Green, OH 43402
419.352.4740

a   *LMN*

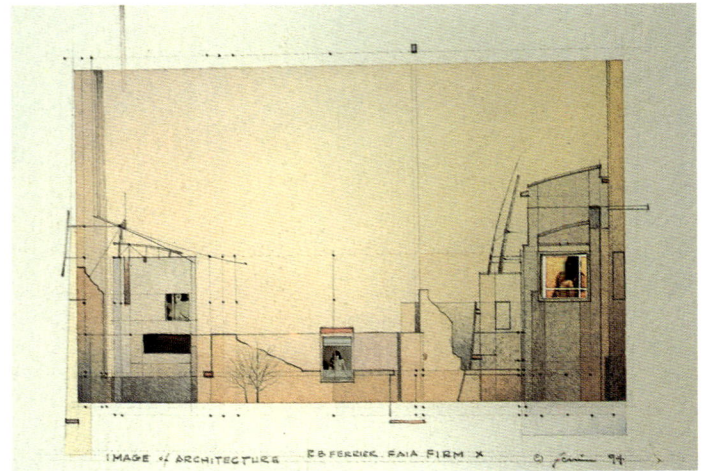

b   *FirmX / Artist*

c   *Keeva J. Kekst Associates*

d **George, Jeffrey Michael**
1800 Pacific Avenue, #108
San Francisco, CA 94109
415.346.6621

e **Gorski, Gilbert, AIA**
Gorski & Associates, P.C.
6633 Spokane Avenue
Lincolnwood, IL 60646
708.329.1340

f **Grealy, Jane**
Jane Grealy & Associates
7.322 Old Cleveland Road
Coorparoo, QLD 4151
Australia
617.394.4333

d *The Redevelopment Agency of the City of San Jose*

e *Ellerbe Becket, Santa Monica*

f *Lambert Smith Architects*

a **Grice, Gordon, OAA, MRAIC**
35 Church Street, #205
Toronto, ONT M5E 1T3
Canada
416.536.9191

b **Grubbs, Christopher**
Christopher Grubbs Illustrator
601 Fourth Street, Loft 102
San Francisco, CA 94107
415.243.4394

c **Hawkins, John A., AIA**
630 Walnut Street
Jeffersonville, IN 47130
812.282.9554

86

b   *Hargreaves Associates*

c   *Nolan & Nolan*

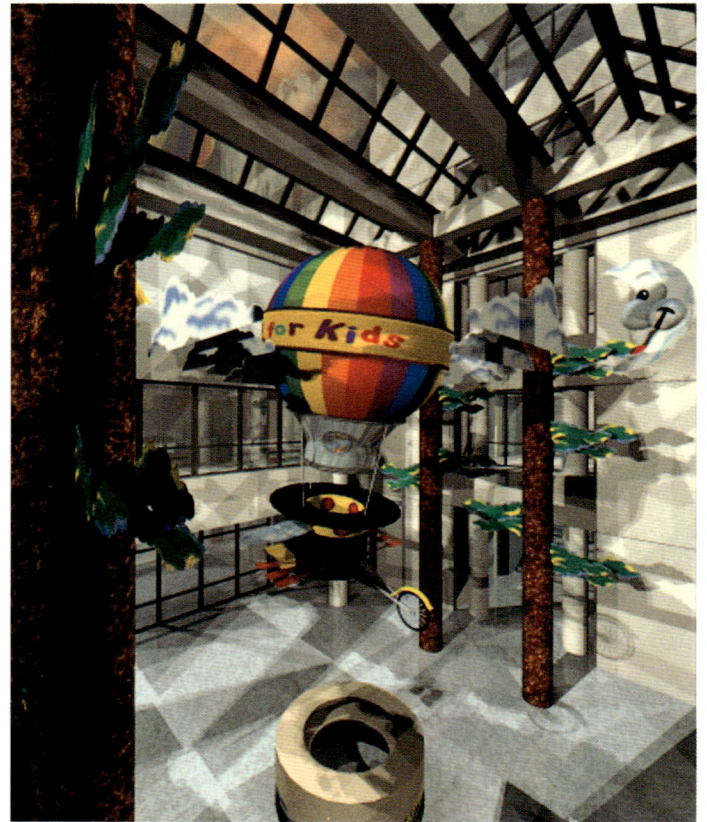

a
Moriyama & Teshima Architects

d **Hayashi, Tomomi**
Shimizuburka
2.130 Higashisonoda-cho
Amagasaki, Hyogo 661
Japan
06.498.5735

e **Hoffpauir, Stephan, AIA**
640 Walavista Avenue
Oakland, CA 94610
510.272.9794

f **Hood, Sallie A.**
Sakal & Hood:
Architecture & Urban Design
1012 Colley Avenue
Norfolk, VA 23507
804.622.6991

e

Karl T. Korth James Sunseri, Architects

d

Takenaka Corporation

f

Sakal and Hood Architects

a **Hook, William**
1501 Western Avenue
Suite 500A
Seattle, WA 98101
206.622.3849

b **Huizing, Howard**
145 South Olive Street
Orange, CA 92666
714.532.3012

c **Ideno, Yoshie**
707 NK kojimachi Quarters
7.10 Sanbancho
Chiyoda-ku, Tokyo 102
Japan
03.3263.4813

c

Akira, Tsuchida

b

a

Stephen Sullivan Architects

d **Jamieson, Douglas E.**
1162 Charm Acres Place
Pacific Pal sades, CA 90272
310.573.1155

e **Joyner, David**
Presentation Techniques
PO Box 11173
Knoxville, TN 37939.1173
615.584.8334

f **Kamiya, Noriko**
Takenaka Corporation
4.9.6 Futamuradai
Toyoake, Aiehi 470.11
Japan
0562.92.0203

d

Zeidler Roberts Partnership

e

Barber & McMurry

f

Takenaka Corporation

a **Kim, Choong-Jin**
Room, #505 (Pusan Dept)
1.1 Dong Kwang-Dong
Jung-Ku, Pusan 600.021
South Korea
051.245.7333

b **Kinuta, Sadako**
Takenaka Corporation
C.7.503, 1-Chome
Nakatomigaoka
Nara-shi, Nara 630
Japan
0742.47.7683

c **Knight, Joseph**
Rosser International
524 West Peachtree Street
Atlanta, GA 30308
404.876.3800

a

Seo-Kang Jong Hap Architects

b

Arata Isozaki & Takenaka Corporation

c

artist / Rosser International

d **Konishi, Hisao**
741.908 Iwakami-dori
Rokkakusagaru
Nakagyo-Ku, Kyoto 604
Japan
075.802.2291

e **Kono, Yoshio**
Takenaka Corporation
4.13, 3-Chome Kamirenjaku
Mitaka-shi, Tokyo 181
Japan
0422.42.3795

f **Kullayanavisut, Visut**
1035 West Lusher Avenue
Elkhart, IN 46517
219.293.0008

d

Atsushi Ueda Architect & Associates

e

Takenaka Corporation

f

a **Larson, Jon**
2339 10th Street
Berkeley, CA 94710
510.204.9346

b **Lee, Sun-Ho**
Suk Jun Building, #601
364.31 Seogko-Dong
Mapo-Ku, Seoul
Korea
02.334.2118x7090

c **Linn, Laura Clayton**
HOK Illustration
211 North Broadway, Suite 600
St. Louis, MO 63102.2733
314.421.2000

a

Jarvis Architects

b

Jung Lim Architects & Engineers

c

Hellmuth Obata & Kassabaum

d **Love, Ronald J.**
Ronald J. Love:
Architectural Illustration
3891 Bayridge Avenue
West Vancouver, BC V7V 3J3
Canada
604.922 3033

e **Maggiore, Ray**
Archetype
138 West 19th Street, #1C
New York, NY 10011
516.621.4772

f **Magyar, Peter**
Spaceprint, Inc.
632 Beaumont Drive
State College, PA 16801
814.466.3054

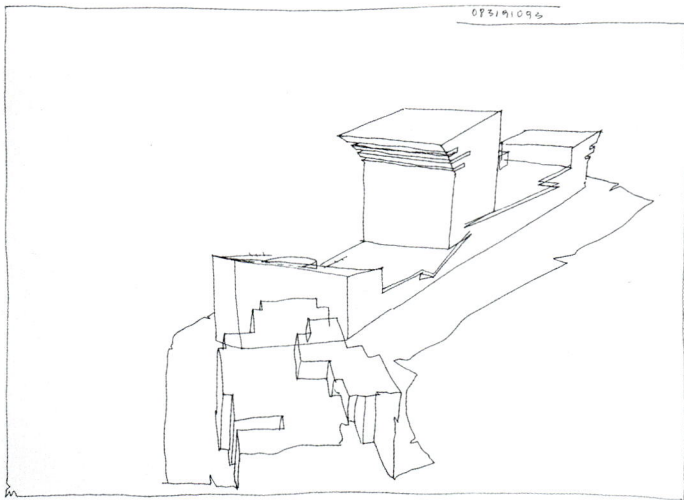

f

L.D. Astorino Architects

d

Paul Merrick Architects

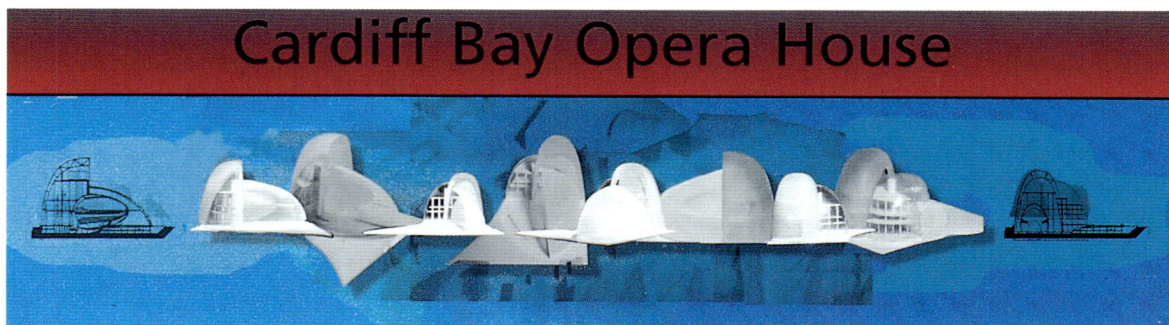

Cardiff Bay Opera House

e

a **Mamiya, Sachiko**
  Takenaka Corporation
  Kohee 1-B 11.1 Rokunotsubo-Cho
  Matsugasaki Sakyo-ku, Kyoto 606
  Japan
  075.791.3536

b **Margolis, John**
  Margolis, Inc.
  380 Boylston Street
  Boston, MA 02116
  508.470.3860

c **Martyniak, Philippe**
  13 Quai Du Commerce
  Lyon 69009
  France
  33.78.64.83.59

a

Takenaka Corporation

b

c

Arata Isozaki & Gimbert Vergel

d **Matsuda, Yasuko**
5.21.6, Katsutadai
Yachiyo, Chiba 276
Japan
0474.83.8574

e **McBride, William A.**
WAM Architectural Illustration
3518 Genessee, Suite 2
South, Kansas City, MO
816.756.0378

f **McIlhargey, Robert**
1639 West 2nd Avenue, #410
Vancouver, BC V6J 1H3
Canada
604.736.7897

e

Moody/Nolan Ltd ./ The Sports Management Group

d

Takenaka Corporation

f

Arthur Erickson, Aitken Wreglesworth

a **Mochizuki, Ayako**
Takenaka Corporation
13.204 Nishiisya-danchi
1.19 Kameooi
Meito-ku, Nagoya, Aichi 465
Japan
052.701.4235

b **Morrissey, Michael**
223 Indian Road Crescent
Toronto, ONT M6P 2G6
Canada
416.763.1387

c **Mullen, Richard**
Presentation Art
203 West Holly Street
Suite 223
Bellingham, WA 98225
360.676.5352

a
Takenaka Corporation

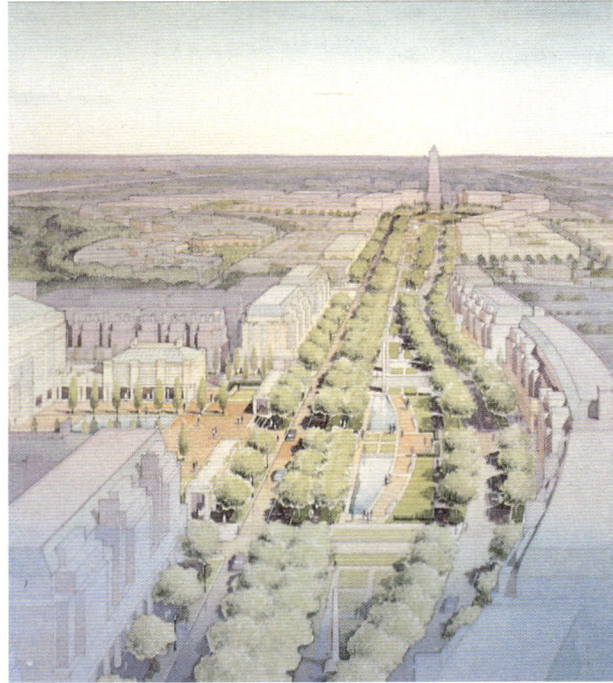

b
Duany Plater-Zyberk Architects & Town Planners

c
Architects Group, Donald Wilcox Architect

d **Nobles, David**
Impulse Images & Animations
9310 Autumn Sunrise
San Antonio, TX 78250
210.521.7221

e **Nodzykowski, Andrew, MRIAC**
3152 Canfield Crescent
N. Vancouver, BC V7R 2V8
Canada
604.980.8339

f **Nojima, Michiko**
F131 Kosumo Kameid Bunka
205, 17.1 2-Chome Bunka
Sumida-Ku, Tokyo 131
Japan
03.3616.1287

e

Alphonse Kho Architect

d

Wiedeman Architects

f

a **O'Beirne, Michael**
42 Eighth Street, #5213
Boston, MA 02129
617.241.8029

b **Ogasawara, Shigeru**
3.6.10.301 Kouenji Minami
Suginamiku, Tokyo 166
Japan
03.3315.4569

c **Oles, Paul Stevenson, FAIA**
Interface Architects
One Gateway Center
Suite 501A
Newton, MA 02158
617.527.6790

ARCHITECTURE IN PERSPECTIVE 10

b

Nobutaka Sasaki

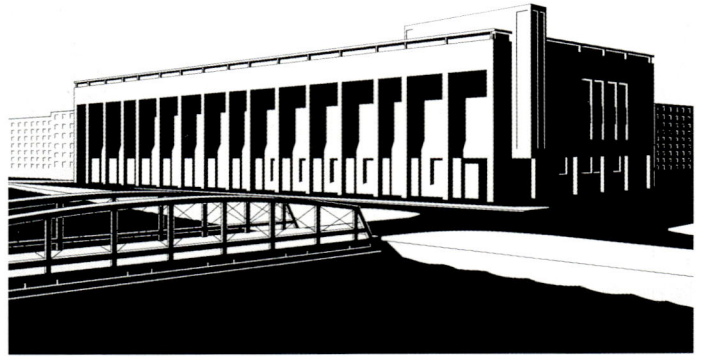

a

Leers, Weinzapfel Associates

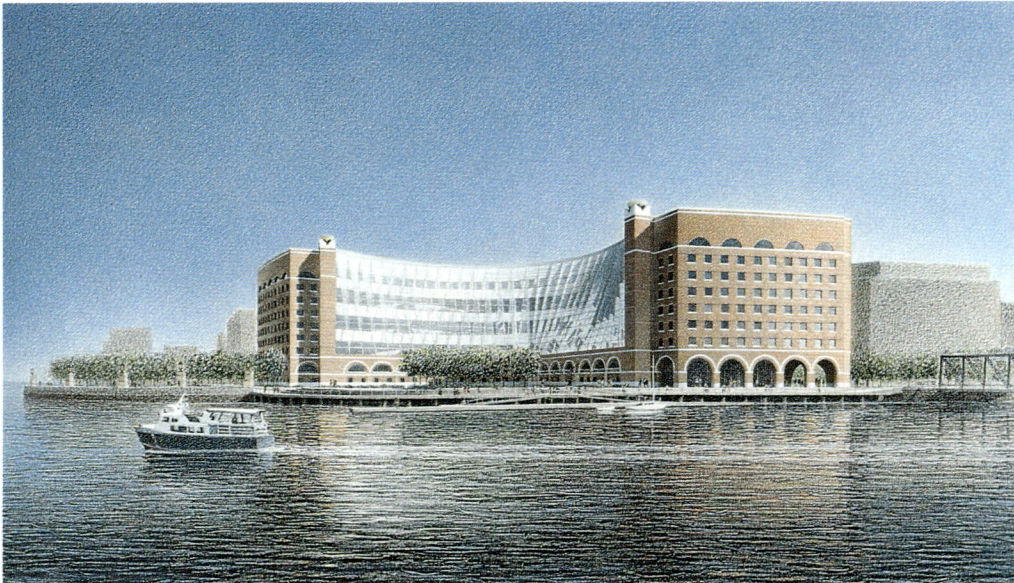

c

Pei, Cobb, Freed & Partners

d **Orest Associates**
3757 Main Highway
PO Box 378
Miami, FL 33133
305.446.8159

e **Ostergaard, Paul, AIA**
UDA Architects
1133 Penn Avenue
Pittsburgh, PA 15222
412.765.1133

f **Ozawa, Kaori**
3.6.10.301 Kouenji Minami
Suginamiku, Tokyo 166
Japan
03.3315.4569

d

e

UDA Architects

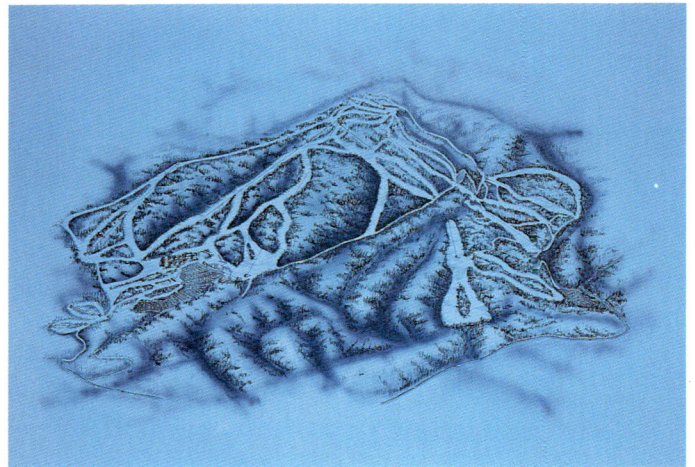

f

EN Design Company

a **Parker, Stephen**
  Hellmuth, Obata & Kassabaum
  211 North Broadway, Suite 600
  St Louis, MO 63102.2733
  314.421.2000

b **Radvenis, Eugene**
  410.1639 West 2nd Avenue
  Vancouver, BC V6J 1H3
  Canada
  604.736.5430

c **Ratner, Barbara Worth, AIA**
  Architectural Illustration
  828 Charles Allen Drive NE
  Atlanta, GA 30308
  404.876.3943

a
Hellmuth Obata Kassabaum

b
Arthur Erickson / Aitken Wreglesworth Architects

c
Space Design International

d **Reardon, Michael**
5433 Boyd Avenue
Oakland, CA 94618
510.655.7030

e **Ringman, Samuel C.**
Ringman Design and Illustration
1800 McKinney Avenue
Dallas, TX 75201
214.871.9001

f **Rosner, Joyce**
The Rosner Studio
4916 Kelvin Street, #2
Houston, TX 77005
713.528.5446

d
Polshek and Partners

e
Elby S. Martin & Associates

SLEDGE RESIDENCE

f
Sharon Tyler Hoover

a **Saito, Ryuichi**
Takenaka Corporation
21.1 8-Chome, Ginza
Chuo-Ku, Tokyo 104
Japan
03.3542.7100

b **Sampson, Philip**
Leo A. Daly
8600 Indian Hills Drive
Omaha, NE 68114
402.391.8111

c **Schaller, Thomas Wells, AIA**
Schaller Architectural
Illustration
2112 Broadway, Suite 407
New York, NY 10023
212.362.5524

a

Takenaka Corporation

b

Leo A. Daly

c

d **Schleef, Eric**
Eric Schleef Illustration
7740 Dean Road
Indianapolis, IN 46240
317.595.0016

e **Scott, Jack**
899 South Plymouth Court
Suite #609
Chicago, IL 60605.2043
312.922.1467

f **Shaw, Tracey**
Jane Grealy & Associates
7/322 Old Cleveland Road
Coorparoo, Brisbane, QLD 4151
Australia
617.394.4333

e

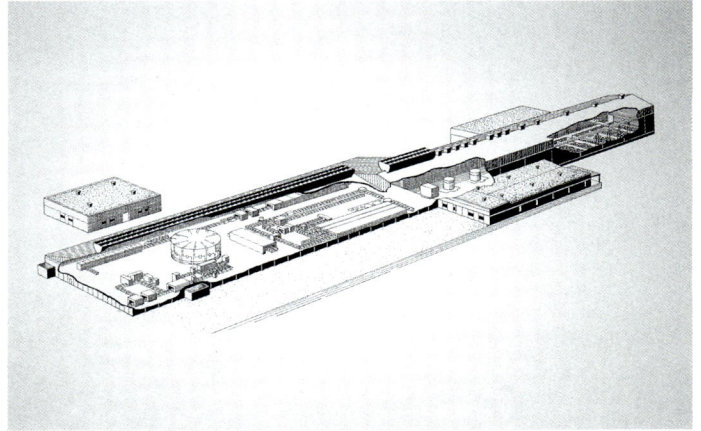
d

HNTB Corporation

f

Peddle Thorp Architects

a **Sherrill, Thomas G.**
Caperton, Johnson, Inc.
14860 Montfort, Suite 200
Dallas, TX 75240
214.991.7082

b **Shirai, Hideo**
31.8.213 Honcho
Wako-shi, Saitama-Ken 351.01
Japan
0484.65.1615

c **Shoda, Hisae**
Takenaka Corporation
8.24.305, 2-Chome Deguchi
Hirakata-shi, Osaka 573
Japan
0720.35.2690

c

Takenaka Corporation

a

Caperton-Johnson

b

Taisei Corporation

d **Slutsky, Rael D., AIA**
Rael D. Slutsky & Associates
8 South Michigan Avenue
Suite 310
Chicago, IL 60603
312.580.1995

e **Smith, James**
700 South Clinton Street
Chicago, IL 60607
312.987.0132

f **Sneary, Richard**
Sneary Architectural Illustration
9728 Overhill Road
Kansas City, MO 64134
816.765.7841

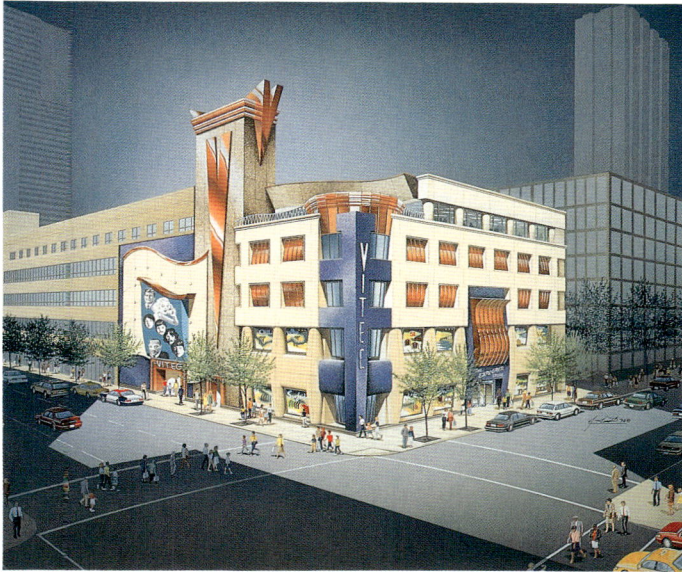

e

Jordan Mozer

f

HOK Sports Facilities Group

d

Skidmore, Owings & Merrill Chicago

a **Szroborz, Stanislaw**
Atelier Szroborz
Merowingerstr. 120
Dusseldorf 40225
Germany
0211.317.96.93

b **Tainer, Dario AIA**
Tainer Assoiciates, LTD.
445 West Erie Street
Chicago, IL 60610
312.951.1656

c **Takahata, Masakazu**
Takenaka Corporation
1.38.21 Kuzuha Noda
Hirakata-shi, Osaka 573
Japan
0720.57.4044

a

b   *Tainer Associates LTD*

c   *Takenaka Corporation*

d **Tansantisuk, Mongkol, AIA**
672 Grove Street
Newton Lower Falls, MA 02162
617.332.7885

e **Tchoban, Sergei**
NPS und Partner
Ulmenstrasse 40
22299 Hamburg
Germany
49.40.48061848

f **Tokita, Keiko**
983.9 Kouwaen
Kuwana, Mie 511
Japan
0594.22.6460

e

Nietz, Prasch, Sigl und Partner Architekten BDA

f

Takenaka Corporation

d

The Stubbins Associates

a **Tolon, Canan**
Tolon Design
814 Camelia Street
Berkeley, CA 94710
510.528.3007

b **Tsurumaki, Akihide**
19.14.201 2-Chome
Kichijoji-Kitamachi
Musasino-shi, Tokyo 180
Japan
0422.201.77

c **van den Hoed, Willem**
1000 HUIZEN
Lange Geer 44
Delft 2611 PW
Holland
3115.133382

a

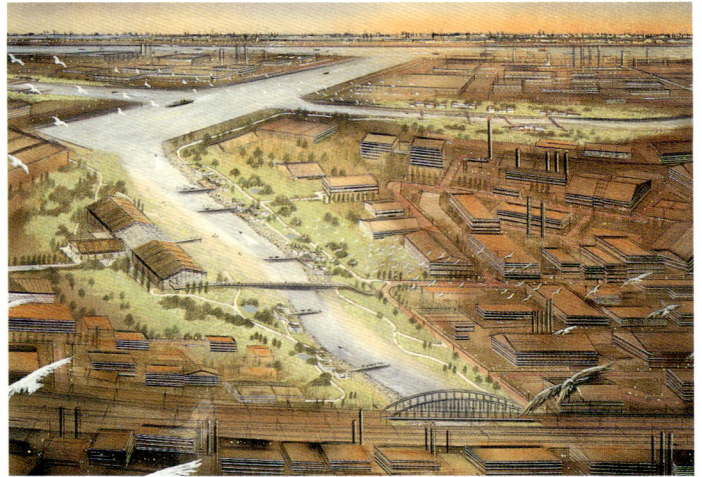

b

Takenaka Corporation

c

Rau & Partners

d **Vangreen, Walter**
  81 Irving Place, #14A
  New York, NY 10003.2217
  212.420.0042

e **Wakita, Masanari**
  Takenaka Corporation
  1.26 Higashiyamamoto-machi
  Chikusa, Nagoya, Aichi 464
  Japan
  052.781.4474

f **Watanabe, Koji**
  2.20.3, Ibukino
  Izumi-shi, Osaka 594
  Japan
  0725.56.7608

d
Charles T. Young Architects

e
Takenaka Corporation

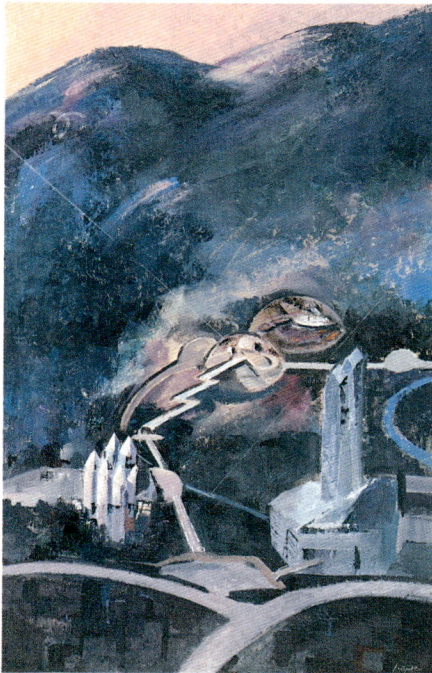

f
Takenaka Corporation

a **Weaver, Ralph**
Ralph Weaver Delineator
RD 1, Box 141
McVeytown, PA 17051
717.899.6985

b **White, Wendy**
McIlhargey/Brown
1639 West 2nd Avenue, #410
Vancouver, BC V6J 1H3
Canada
604.736.7897

c **Woodhouse, Curtis James**
4141 Lybyer Avenue
Miami, FL 33133
305.663.8347

b

Perkins & Co. Architects

a

c

d **Yamada, Kunio**
Lions Mansion
Kak-2.9 Kikusaka-cho Chik-ku
Nagoya, Aichi 464
Japan
052.751.3811

e **Yamamoto, Tamotsu**
15 Sleeper Street
Boston, MA 02210
617.542.1021

f **Yanagida, Emiko**
Hara Bldg 4F, 3.13.1 Hizoo
Sibuya-ku, Tokyo 150
Japan
03.3400.0371

f *Fumio Shimizu Architect*

e *Skidmore Owings & Merrill*

d

a **Yamamoto, Tamotsu**
   15 Sleeper Street
   Boston, MA 02210
   617.542.1021

b **Zaleski, Serge, ARAIA**
   Delineation Graphix
   238 Bulwara Road, Ultimo
   Sydney, NSW 2007
   Australia
   61.2.552.3666

c **Zimmerman, Aaron**
   120 N.W. Parkway
   Kansas City, MO 64150
   816.587.9500

b

Keane Murphy and Duff, Architects

c

WRS

a

The Hugh Ferriss Memorial Prize, awarded annually for excellence in the graphic representation of architecture, is sustained by the continued sponsorship of the Van Nostrand Reinhold Company, New York City.

a **Dunnette, Lee, AIA**
430 East 20th Street, #5B
New York, NY 10009
212.260.4240
AIP [1]

b **Record, James**
AIP 1

a

b

a **Lovelace, Richard**
AIP 2

b **Schaller, Thomas Wells, AIA**
Schaller Architectural Illustration
2112 Broadway, Suite 407
New York, NY 10023
212.362.5524
AIP 3

a

b

c **Willis, Daniel, AIA**
1921 North Oak Lane
State College, PA 16803
814.867.5459
AIP 4

d **Gorski, Gilbert, AIA**
Gorski & Associates, P.C.
6633 Spokane Avenue
Lincolnwood, IL 60646
708.329.1340
AIP 5

c

Willis, Daniel, AIA

d

a **Blanc, Luis**
30 St. Felix Street, #2B
Brooklyn, NY 11217
718.797.1267
AIP 6

b **Jamieson, Douglas E.**
1162 Charm Acres Place
Pacific Palisades, CA 90272
310.573.1155
AIP 7

a

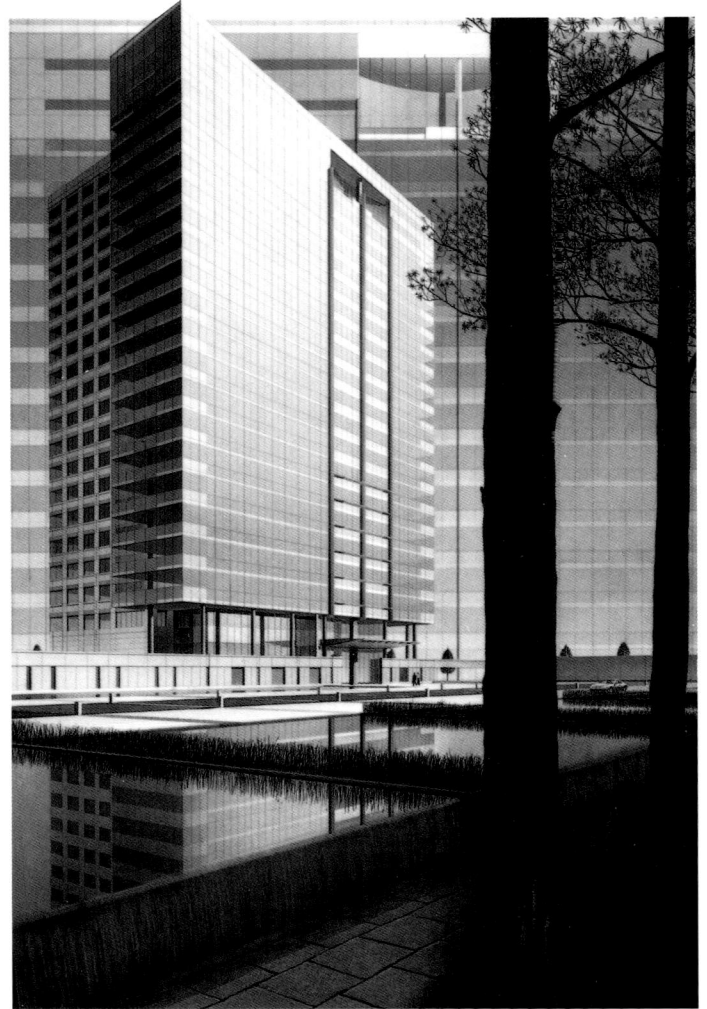

b

c **Sylvester, David**
  Sylvester Illustration
  441 Vannest Avenue
  Trenton, NJ 08618
  609.882.4360
  AIP 8

d **Slutsky, Rael D., AIA**
  Rael D. Slutsky & Associates
  8 South Michigan Avenue, Suite 310
  Chicago, IL 60603
  312.580.1995
  AIP 9

c

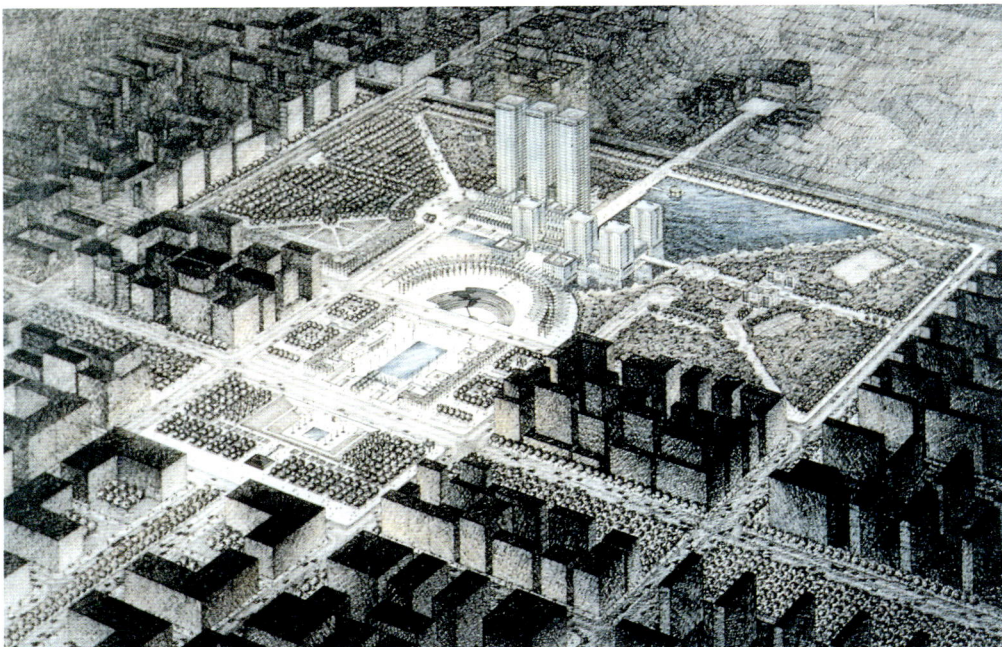

d

c **Sylvester, David**
  Sylvester Illustration
  441 Vannest Avenue
  Trenton, NJ 08618
  609.882.4360
  AIP 8

d **Slutsky, Rael D., AIA**
  Rael D. Slutsky & Associates
  8 South Michigan Avenue, Suite 310
  Chicago, IL 60603
  312.580.1995
  AIP 9

Retrospective

Every year, in order that the exhibition not exceed 60 works, hundreds of drawings must be rejected by the jury. Many of these are exceptional drawings, as indicated in the previous section. They are turned aside with great regret, even anguish, on the part of the jury. The following pages contain a collection of works picked from the non-premiated entries to Architecture in Perspective exhibitions of the past ten years. This work is offered without further comment by the three ASAP founders and has not been previously published in our catalogues.

a **Abbott, Michael**
3471 Via Lido, Suite 201
Newport Beach, CA 92663
714.675.7530
AIP 3

b **Birkey, Randal**
635 South Home Street
Oak Park, IL 60304
708.386.5150
AIP 3

c **Boozer, Ron**
129 West Trade Street
Charlotte, NC 28202
704.377.5941
AIP 5

d **Brown, Lori**
1639 West 2nd Street
Suite 410
Vancouver, BC
Canada V6SIH3
604.736.7897
AIP 8

a

c

b

d

a **Burroughs, Michael**
14342 Sunrise Drive N.E.
Bainbridge Island, WA 98110
206.780.9406
AIP 8

b **Byers, Brent, FAIA**
501 Elm Street
Dallas, TX
214.748.2000
AIP 1

c **Cloud, Gregory**
2116 Arlington Avenue, #236
Los Angeles, CA 90018
213.484.9479
AIP 3

d **Costantino, Frank M.**
13B Pauline Street
Winthrop, MA 02152
617.846.4766
AIP 3

d

b

a

c

e **Cook, Robert**
Prelim Inc.
5477 Glen Lakes Drive
Dallas, TX 75231
214.692.7226
AIP 5

f **Day, Elizabeth A.**
1218 Baylor Street, Suite 204
Austin, TX 78703
512.469.6011
AIP 8

g **Diniz, Carlos**
3529 Deronda Drive
Los Angeles, CA 90068
213.469.7222
AIP 3

h **Doggett, W. Kirk**
One Peary Drive
Brunswick, ME 04011
207.725.3516
AIP 1

e

f

SOUTHERN OCEAN COUNTY HOSPITAL

g

h

a **Duffin, Ken**
18016 NE 28th Street
Redmond, WA 98052
206.885.9300
AIP 4

b **Dunnette, Lee, AIA**
430 East 20th Street, #5B
New York, NY 10009
212.260.4240
AIP 5

c **England, Jennifer**
3757 Main Highway
PO Box 398
Miami, FL 33133
305.446.8159
AIP 8

d **Gorski, Gilbert, AIA**
6633 Spokane Street
Lincolnwood, IL 60646
708.329.1340
AIP 8

124

a

b

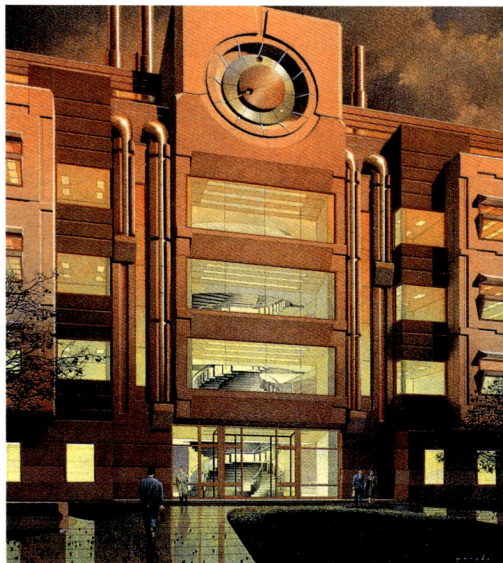

d

c

e **Grubbs, Christopher**
601 4th Street, #102
San Francisco, CA 94107
415.243.4394
AIP 3

f **Gutierrez, Miguelangel**
Av Mazlatan, # 5,
Ent. A, Dept. 4
Col. Condesa, D.F. 06140
Mexico
525.211.1921
AIP 5

g **Hanna, Jack**
348 F.A. Dept of Art
University of Houston
Houston, TX 77204-4893
713.743.2831
AIP 3

h **Harmon, Dan**
2089 McKinley Road, NW
Atlanta, GA 30318
404.609.9330
AIP 3

h

g

f

e

a Hickes, Andy
205 Third Avenue #98
New York, NY 10003
212.677.8054
AIP 5

b Hook, William G.
1501 Western Avenue #500A
Seattle, WA 98101
206.622.3849
AIP 4

c Hyne, Eric
525 Maple Ridge Lane
Odenton, MD 21113
410.551.5405
AIP 5

d Jacques, Wayne John, AIA
39 Church Street
Boston, MA 02116
617.426.2557
AIP 4

a

b

c

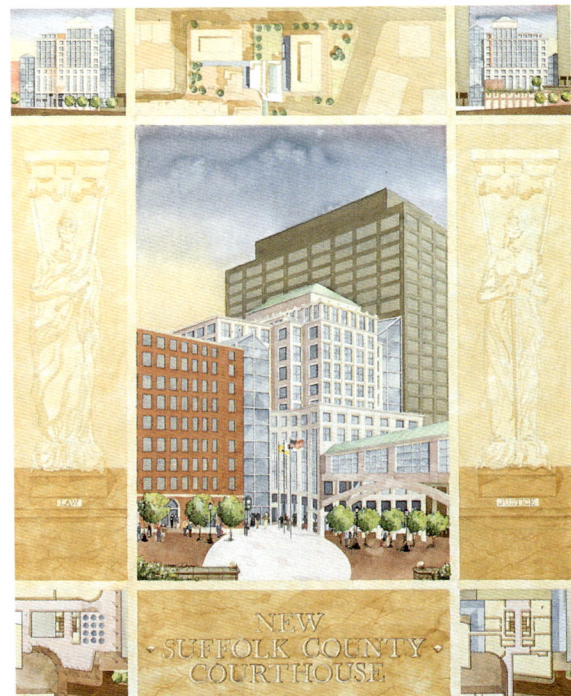

d

e **Konishi, Hisao**
741 908 Iwagami-cho
Rokkaku -Sagaru Iwogamidori
Nakagyo Ku, Kyoto, 604
Japan
81.75.802.2291
AIP

f **Lane, David Mark, AIA**
1187 Coast Village Road
Suite 1.336
Santa Barbara, CA 93108
805.963.7373
AIP 3

g **Lee, Sun-Ho**
Suk Jun Building, #601
364-31 Seogyo-Dong
Mapo-Ku, Seoul
Korea
02.334.2118x7090
AIP 8

h **Lukaitis, Sonya R.**
202 1504 West 14th Avenue
Vancouver, BC
Canada
604.736.5358
AIP 4

g

f

h

e

a **Magruder, William**
980 Bluebird Street
Laguna Beach, CA 92651
714.497.1845
AIP 5

b **Margolis, John**
380 Boylston Street
Boston, MA 02116
617.859.2950
AIP 6

c **McAllen, Bob**
3268 Military Avenue
W. Los Angeles, CA 90034
310.477.8374
AIP 5

d **McCann, Michael**
2 Gibson Avenue
Toronto, Ontario MSR IT5
Canada
416.964.7532
AIP 8

b

c

d

a

e **Mcl argey, Robert**
1639 West 2nd Avenue
Suite #410
Vancouver, BC V6J IH3
Canada
604.736.7897
AIP 3

f **Mead, Syd**
1716 North Gardner Street
Los Angeles, CA 90046
213.850.5225
AIP IV 87

g **Miller, Kenneth**
103 North 38th Street
Belleville, IL 62223
618.234.6172
AIP 4

h **Morrissey, Michael B.**
223 Indian Road Crescent
Toronto, Ontario M6P 2G6
Canada
416.763.1387
AIP 4

i

h

g

e

a **Nobles, David**
9310 Autumn Sunrise
San Antonio, TX 78250
210.521.7221
AIP II 87

b **Oles, Paul Stevenson, FAIA**
One Gateway Center, 501A
Newton, MA 02158
617.527.6790
AIP 8

c **Orest Associates**
3757 Main Highway
PO Box 378
Miami, FL 33133
305.446.8159
AIP 3

d **Parker, Stephen**
HOK Architects, Inc.
211 N. Broadway, #600
St. Louis, MO 63102
314.421.2000
AIP 5

a

b

c

d

e **Patricia, Steven N.**
4671 Peachtree Drive
Murrysville, PA 15668
412.327.8007
AIP 4

f **Pattillo, Charles**
4902 Apache Avenue
Jacksonville, FL 32210
904.384.2293
AIP 3

g **Pearson, Wilbur**
6880 S.W. 98th Street
Miami, FL 33156
305.667.9811
AIP 4

h **Radke, Richard G.**
1350 Shire Circle Drive
Inverness, IL 60067
708.705.7800
AIP 5

f

h

g

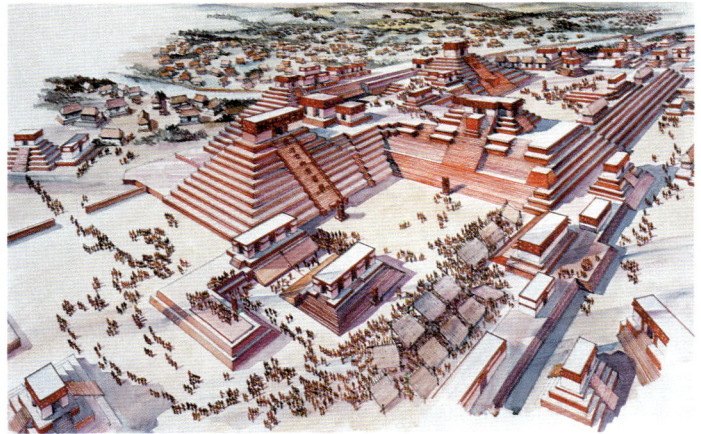

e

a **Radvenis, Eugene**
410-1639 W. 2nd Avenue
Vancouver BC V6J IH3
Canada
604.736.5430
AIP 5

b **Rajkovich, Thomas Norman**
817 Judson Avenue, 1-W
Evanston, IL 60202-2432
708.332.2782
AIP 4

c **Ratner, Barbara Worth, AIA**
828 Charles Allen Drive NE
Atlanta, GA 30308
404.876.3943
AIP 8

d **Reardon, Michael**
5433 Boyd Avenue
Oakland, CA 94618
510.655.7030
AIP 3

c

b

d

a

e **Roe, Harold**
5800 Monroe Street
PO Box 403
Sylvania, OH 43560
419.882.7131
AIP 4

f **Roper, Peter A.G.**
32 Union Boulevard
St. Lambert PQ J4R 2M5
Canada
514.465.1309
AIP 4

g **Rosner, Joyce**
4916 Kelvin Street, #2
Houston, TX 77005
713.528.5446
AIP 8

h **Schaller, Thomas Wells, AIA**
2112 Broadway, Suite 407
New York, NY 10023
212.362.5524
AIP 8

e

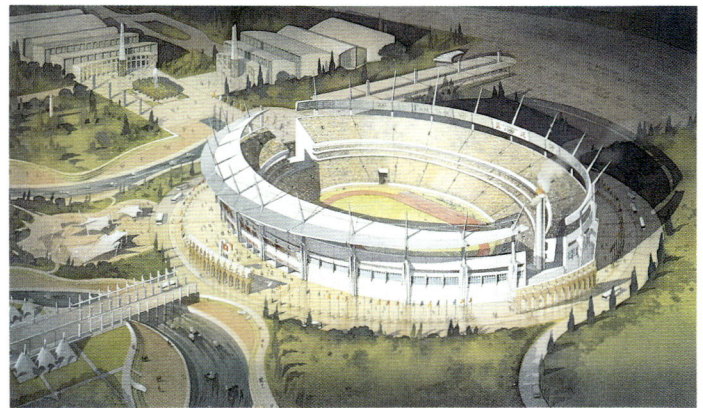

h

f

g

a **Smith, James C.**
700 South Clinton Street
Chicago, IL 60607
312.987.0132
AIP 5

b **Sneary, Richard**
9728 Overhill Road
Kansas City, MO 64134
816.765.7841
AIP 5

c **Sorenson, Henry**
702 South 14th Strret
Bozeman, MT 59715
406.994.4255
AIP 8

d **Stinson, Don**
PO Box 7784
Breckenridge, CO 80424
303.453.0663
AIP 4

a

c

d

b

e **Tainer, Dario, AIA**
Tainer Associates, LTD
445 W. Erie Street, Suite 201
Chicago, IL 60610
312.951.1656
AIP 5

f **Thomas. Peter**
15 Twin Pond Lane
Lincoln, MA 01773
617.259.8946
AIP 2

g **Wang, Sung Ja**
Art Plan, #403, Saeleem Building
1158-5 Cholyang 3Dong Dong-Gu
Pusan, 601-013
Korea
AIP 5

h **Yamamoto, Tamotsu**
15 Sleeper Street
Boston, MA 02210
617.542.1021
AIP 6

h

g

f

e

e **Tainer, Dario, AIA**
Tainer Associates, LTD
445 W. Erie Street, Suite 201
Chicago, IL 60610
312.951.1656
AIP 5

f **Thomas. Peter**
15 Twin Pond Lane
Lincoln, MA 01773
617.259.8946
AIP 2

g **Wang, Sung Ja**
Art Plan, #403, Saeleem Building
1158-5 Cholyang 3Dong Dong-Gu
Pusan, 601-013
Korea
AIP 5

h **Yamamoto, Tamotsu**
15 Sleeper Street
Boston, MA 02210
617.542.1021
AIP 6

Abbott, Joseph 23450 Manistee
Oak Park, MI 48237

Abe, Masaharu Abe Renderings
7.19.22.515 Nishi Shinjuku
Shinjuku-ku, Tokyo, 160
Japan
03.3369.3722, Fax: 03.3369.3787

Advanced Media Design 14 Imperial Place, Suite 202
Providence, RI 02903
401.272.1637

Aizawa, Isao 10.8.15 Nishioka 1 Jo
Toyohiraku, Sapporo-shi, Hokkaido 062
Japan
853.9971, Fax: 011.853.9972

Alessi, Lawrence 72 Seminole
Pontiac, MI 48341

Alvarez, Victor The BJSS Group
320 West Bay Drive, Suite 212
Olympia, WA 98502
206.943.4560

Antwis, Donald 7 Arvon Street
Beachmere, QLD 4510
Australia
074.968645, Fax: 074.968043

Aoki, Yutaka 707NK Kojimachi Quaters
7.10 Sanbancho, Chiyod-ku, Tokyo 102
Japan
03.3263.4813, Fax: 03.3263.5130

Archimation Kantstr 142
Berlin 10623
Germany
049.30.312.1306, Fax: 30.312.1620

Asada, Yoshio 11.23 Tuchibotoke Kawata
Yamashina-ku, Kyoto, Kyoto 607
Japan
075.592.0931, Fax: 075.592.5940

Bader, David Neubau Architects
PO Box 327
Washington Crossing, PA 18977
215.493.4302, Fax: 215.493.4305

Baehr, Richard, AIA 305 Northern Boulevard
Great Neck, NY 11021
516.466.0470, Fax: 516.466.1670

Ball, Daniel 239 West North Broadway
Columbus, OH 43214
614.478.2385, Fax: 614.478.3434

Ballings, Alexander 7ARTS visuals
Mechtildisstraat 2, Tilburg 5021 CN
Holland
31.13.355341, Fax: 31.13.364881

Battersby, Christopher Architectural Illustration
4/F Cina Overseas Bldg
139 Hennessy Road, Wanchai
Hong Kong
852.2821.6406, Fax: 852.2529.6419

Becker, Robert 35 South Broadway N7
Irvington, NY 10533
914.591.5906, Fax: 914.591.5906

Blanc, Luis 30 St. Felix Street, #2B
Brooklyn, NY 11217
718.797.1267, Fax: 718.522.1511

Brinson, J. David, AIA 7948 Goodwood Boulevard
Baton Rouge, LA 70806
504.926.5045, Fax: 504.926.5046

Broland, Kathryn 88 Pendleton Lane
Londonderry, NH 03053
602.432.0736

Brown, Christine 12 Heaslas Strees
Wooloongabba, QLD 4102
Australia
07.891.2307, Fax: 07.891.2615

Brown, J. Melissa 35 Lyme Road
Newton, MA 02165
617.527.6832

Brown, Lori Lori Brown Consultants
410.1639 West 2nd Avenue
Vancouver, BC V6J 1H3
Canada
604.736.7897, Fax: 604.736.9763

Brown, Mona 7 Bonnie Brook Lane
Westport, CT 06880
203.222.8088, Fax: 203.222.0726

Brown, Stephen 110 Lakeview Avenue
Waltham, MA 02154
617.367.6300, Fax: 617.742.8722

Buccalo, Nicholas Joel The Drawing Studio
211 Warren Street
Brooklyn, NY 11201
718.488.7894, Fax: 718.488.7894

Buchanan, Edward 5825 Keith Avenue, #4
Oakland, CA 94618
510.654.6755, Fax: 510.654.3424

Burroughs, Michael 14342 Sunrise Drive NE
Bainbridge Island, WA 98110
206.780.9406

Cermak, Dianne, S.P. 34 Glendoon Road
Needham, MA 02192
617.455.6334

Cernik, Carol Wedmeyer, Cernik, Corrubia
314 N. Broadway, Suite 858
St. Louis, MO 63102
314.231.9377, Fax: 314.231.9009

Chao, Hans 222 Commonwealth Avenue, #3.R
Boston, MA 02116
617.492.7000

Chen, John, S.M., AIA Howard U. Architecture Dept.
12505 Montclair Drive
Silver Springs, MD 20904
202.636.7430

Chenoweth, Richard 518 Margaret Drive
Silver Springs, MD 20910
301.588.0528, Fax: 301.589.0336

Chinen, Makoto 203 Diapalace Yagotoomoteyam 2.401
Omoteyama Tenpa, Nagoya, Aichi 468
Japan
052.834.7033, Fax: 052.834.7033

Chiodini, Elaine, CPAA
121 South Estes Drive, #100
PO Box 2268
Chapel Hill, NC 27515
919.092.907158, Fax: 919.942.7535

Chubachi, Sachiko 563 Ishiyama Minami-ku
Sapporo-shi, Sapporo 005
Japan
591.1683, Fax: 011.591.9519

Church, Ron 21211 West Ten Mile Road, #702
Southfield, MI 48075

City of Las Vegas Office of Architectural Services
400 East Stewart Avenue
Las Vegas, NV 89101
702.229.6535, Fax: 702.382.3232

Clary, Laura 1040 Springfield
Northville, MI 48167

Clement, Norma Lund Associates
1621 Sheridan Lake Road
Rapid City, SD 50772
605.348.6254, Fax: 605.348.3555

Cocke, John 625 Trapelo Road
Belmont, MA 02178
617.489.5407

Coleman, Neil Ernest 97 Hadfield Street
Birkenhead, Auckland
New Zealand
09.4835.018, Fax: 09.4835.018

Comazzi, Robert Sasaki Associates
64 Pleasant Street
Watertown, MA 02172
617.926.3300, Fax: 617.924.2748

Costantino, Frank M. F.M. Costantino, Inc.
13B Pauline Street
Winthrop, MA 02152
617.846.4766, Fax: 617.846.4766

Cruse, James, III 1046 Seyburn
Detroit, MI 48214

Dabrowska, Alina 822, 3130, 66 Avenue SW
Calgary, ALB T3E 5K8
Canada
403.249.7008

Day, Elizabeth Ann 1218 Baylor Street, #204
Austin, TX 78703
512.469.6011, Fax: 512.469.6020

De la Paz, Dennis 501 Elm, Suite 500
Dallas, TX 75202
214.748.2000, Fax: 214.653.8281

De Lara, Edgardo, A. Hellmuth, Obata & Kassabaum
6688 N. Central Expwy, Suite 700
Dallas, TX 75206
214.739.6688, Fax: 214.373.9523

DeCastro, Angelo Rua Do Alto Da Milha, 50
Sao Joao Do Estoril 2765
Portugal
351.1.4671010, Fax: 351.1.4661648

DeGuzman, Emmanuel Noni Architectural Perspectives
1531 Delmar Avenue
Kissimmee, FL 34744
407.933.5219, Fax: 407.933.5219

DeJesus, Rafael 306, 229.11th Avenue SE
Calgary, ALB T2G 0Y1
Canada
403.265.3304, Fax: 403.266.1992

Diamond, A.J. A.J. Diamond, Donald Schmitt
2 Berkeley Street, Suite 600
Toronto, ONT M5A 2N3
Canada
416.862.8800, Fax: 416.862.5508

Dilger, Curt Neubau Imaging
1313 Lord Sterling Road, Box 327
Washington Crossing, PA 18977
215.493.4302, Fax: 215.493.4305

Diniz, Carlos 3259 Deronda Drive
Los Angeles, CA 90068.1609
213.469.7222, Fax: 213.469.2026

DiVito, Kenneth 4347 Devonshire Drive
Troy, MI 48098
313.952.5155, Fax: 810.952.5155

Djohan, Ferry JL.X(EKS) No.23 Rt.05/010 Kebonbaru
Tebet, Jakarta 12830
Indonesia
62.21.828.0681, Fax: 62.21.828.0681

Do, Tung, Th. GMB Architects & Engineers
PO Box 2159
Holland, MI 49422.2159
616.392.7034, Fax: 616.392.2677

Doctor, Stanley 747 Poplar Avenue
Boulder, CO 80304
303.449.3259, Fax: 303.449.0629

Dong, Wei 1300 Linden Drive
Madison, WI 53706
608.262.8805, Fax: 608.262.5335

Dukett, Andrew 496 Midland Park Drive
Stone Mountain, GA 30087
404.564.0342, Fax: 404.364.0064

Dunnette, Lee, AIA 430 East 20th Street, #5B
New York, NY 10009
212.260.4240, Fax: 212.353.2305

Durante, Dominick, Jr. City Architecture
3311 Perkins Avenue
Cleveland, OH 44115
216.881.2444, Fax: 216.881.6713

Dwyer, Michael, AIA Butterick, White & Burtis
475 Tenth Avenue
New York, NY 10018
212.967.3333, Fax: 212.629.3749

Earl, James 17 Parkview Drive
Hingham, MA 02043
617.749.7982

Edgeley, Peter, FASI, RIBA Peter Edgeley PTY LTD
30 Queens Road, Suite 17
Melbourne, Victoria 3004
Australia
613.9866.6620, Fax: 613.9866.6621

Elabd, Samir Truex deGroot Collins Architects
209 Battery Street
Burlington, VT 05401
802.658.2775

Endom, Charles d/b/a Charles Endom Illustrator
256 Macarthur Avenue
Pittsburg, CA 94565
510.432.9397

Estor, Ramon 2140 East Hacienda Avenue
Las Vegas, NV 89119
702.795.0906

Evans, Bill 714 1st Avenue West
Seattle, WA 98119
206.282.8785, Fax: 206.282.8764

Evans, George 6517 Shady Valley Drive
Flowery Branch, GA 30542

Farnsworth, Craig Johnson, Johnson and Roy
30 West Monroe Street, Suite 1010
Chicago, IL 60603
312.641.0770, Fax: 312.641.6728

Ferrier, Richard, FAIA FIRM X Ferrier, Hampton, Quevedo, King
1628 Connally Terrace
Arlington, TX 76010
817.469.8605, Fax: 817.794.5094

Fleming, Dudley Rockwood Sumner Grant
136 1/2 South Main Street, Studio 1
Bowling Green, OH 43402
419.352.4740, Fax: 419.353.4576

Fox, L. David 1715 Volunteer Boulevard
Knoxville, TN 37996.2400
615.974.5265, Fax: 615.974.0656

Fritz, Steve 1815 East Front Street
Traverse City, MI 49686
616.947.3059, Fax: 616.947.7669

Fyfe, Sean 2970 South 300 East, #1
South Salt Lake, UT 84115
801.484.6535

Gagne, Dave 340A, rue Cousineau
Laval, QUE H7G 3K1
Canada
504.663.8612

Garnett, Ronald The Haskell Company
11635 Sedgemore Drive South
Jacksonville, FL 32223
904.791.4500, Fax: 904.791.4697

George, Jeffrey 1800 Pacific Avenue, #108
San Francisco, CA 94109
415.346.6621

Genesis Studios Inc. 225 South Swoope Avenue, #205
Maitland, FL 32751
407.539.2606, Fax: 407.644.7901

Gohl, Roger Interior Design Delineation
2643 Stoner Avenue
Los Angeles, CA 90064
310.479.0754

Gorski, Gilbert, AIA Gorski & Associates, P.C.
6633 Spokane Avenue
Lincolnwood, IL 60646
708.329.1340, Fax: 708.329.9321

Grealy, Jane Jane Grealy & Associates PTY LTD
7.322 Old Cleveland Road
Coorparoo, QLD 4151
Australia
617.394.4333, Fax: 617.849.0646

Grice, Gordon, OAA, MRAIC 35 Church Street, #205
Toronto, ONT M5E 1T3
Canada
416.536.9191, Fax: 416.696.8866

Grossi, Jason 2705 Jos. St. Louis Avenue
Windsor, ONT N8T 2M7
Canada

Grubbs, Christopher Christopher Grubbs Illustrator
601 Fourth Street, Loft 102
San Francisco, CA 94107
415.243.4394, Fax: 415.243.4395

Gutierrez, Miguelangel AV. Mazatlan No. 5 Edif. A Ent. A
Depto. 4 Col. Condesa, DF 06140
Mexico
525.211.1921, Fax:011.525.553.2169

Hamersky, Bohdan PO Box 204/41 Horne Tooke Road
Palisades, NY 10964
212.675.0400, Fax: 212.620.4687

Harmon, Dan Dan Harmon & Associates
2089 McKinley Road NW
Atlanta, GA 30318
404.609.9330, Fax: 404.609.9308

Hasegawa, Kazuo K. A. Design
ACA Building 3.7.25 Marunouchi Naka-ku
Nagoya, Aichi 460
Japan
052.971.3171, Fax: 052.971.3250

Hausher, Gerald East-West Illustrators
P.H. 2222 Kalakaua Avenue
Honolulu, HI 96815
808.924.3609

Hawkins, John A., AIA 630 Walnut Street
Jeffersonville, IN 47130
812.282.9554, Fax:812.282.9171

Hayashi, Tomomi Shimizubunka
2.130 Higashisonoda-cho
Amagasaki, Hyogo 661
Japan
06.498.5735

Heiderer, Erik 13738 Bayview
Sterling Heights, MI 48310

Henry, Larry, AIA Architectural fx
309 West Pueblo Street
Reno, NV 89509
702.786.1011, Fax:702.786.1334

Hickes, Andy 205 Third Avenue, #98
New York, NY 10003
212.677.8054, Fax: 212.677.8054

Hoffpauir, Stephan, AIA 640 Walavista Avenue
Oakland, CA 94610
510.272.9794, Fax: 510.272.9794

Holly, Brent 37849 Lakeshore Drive
Harrison Turnpike, MI 4
810.465.7912

Hood, Sallie A. Sakal & Hood: Architecture & Urban Design
1012 Colley Avenue
Norfolk, VA 23507
804.622.6991

Hook, William 1501 Western Avenue, Suite 500A
Seattle, WA 98101
206.622.3849, Fax: 206.624.1494

Huf, Peter Muehlenweg 1
Hartenfels 56244
Germany
49.2626.7610, Fax: 49.2626.761103

Huizing, Howard 145 South Olive Street
Orange, CA 92666
714.532.3012, Fax: 714.532.5298

Hyne, Eric 525 Maple Ridge Lane
Odenton, MD 21113
410.551.5405, Fax: 410.551.5405

Ideno, Yoshie 707 NK kojimachi Quarters
7.10 Sanbancho
Chiyoda-ku, Tokyo 102
Japan
03.3263.4813, Fax: 03.3263.5130

Ishida, Chiaki 81.6 Higashi-1, Inada
Obihiro, Hokkaido 080
Japan
0155.48.8511, Fax: 0155.48.8511

Jacques, Wayne John, AIA Warren Freedenfeld & Associates
39 Church Street
Boston, MA 02116
617.338.0050, Fax: 617.426.2557

Jamieson, Douglas E. 1162 Charm Acres Place
Pacific Palisades, CA 90272
310.573.1155, Fax:310.459.1429

Javier, Joel 2801 Walnut Bend Lane, #321
Houston, TX 77042
713.782.5392, Fax: 713.782.5392

Jimenez, Angelito Altares PO Box 528 MPC 3705
Berakas Old Airport, Band. Seri Beg.
3580 Brunei

Johnson, Richard 4105 178th Lane SE, #305
Bellevue, WA 98008

Joyner, David Presentation Techniques
PO Box 11173
Knoxville, TN 37939.1173
615.584.8334, Fax: 615.584.8334

Kadowaki, Nobuo KVC Inc.
Wakamathu Bldg, 3.23.10, Sendagaya
Shibuya-ku, Tokyo 051
Japan
3.3401.5877, Fax: 3.3402.7185

Kamezaki, Toshiro 11.246 Shiokusa Cho
Seto City, Aichi 489
Japan
0561.83.3046

Kamiya, Noriko Takenaka Corporation
4.9.6 Futamuradai
Toyoake, Aiehi 470.11
Japan
0562.92.0203

Kariya, Takuji 1.5.5.3405 Tomobuchi-cho
Miyakojima-Ku, Osaka 534
Japan
06.924.3637, Fax: 06.924.3287

Ki, Young 270 Washington Boulevard
Hoffman Estates, IL 60194
708.843.3389, Fax: 312.580.1980

Kim, Choong-Jin Room, #505 (Pusan Dept)
1.1 Dong Kwang-Dong
Jung-Ku, Pusan 600.021
South Korea
051.245.7333, Fax: 051.245.0057

Kindred, Garfield 18557 Canal Road, #3,
Clinton Township, MI 48038.5821
313.263.7830, Fax: 313.263.7832

Kingston, Ray 132 Pierpoint Avenue, Suite 200
Salt Lake City, UT 84101

Kinsey, Steve Kinsey Associates
2509 Sylvania Avenue
Toledo, OH 43613
419.475.7011, Fax: 419.475.7262

Kinuta, Sadako Takenaka Corporation
C.7.503, 1-Chome Nakatomigaoka
Nara-shi, Nara 630
Japan
0742.47.7683

Knight, Joseph Rosser International
524 West Peachtree Street
Atlanta, GA 30308
404.876.3800, Fax: 404.888.7229

Konishi, Hisao 741.908 Iwakami-dori Rokkakusagaru
Nakagyo-Ku, Kyoto 604
Japan
81.75.802.2291, Fax: 81.75.802.5112

Kono, Yoshio Takenaka Corporation
4.13, 3-Chome Kamirenjaku
Mitaka-shi, Tokyo 181
Japan
0422.42.3795

Kullayanavisut, Visut 1035 West Lusher Avenue
Elkhart, IN 46517
219.293.0008, Fax: 219.293.7712

La, An. S., 12 Landale Street Box Hill 3128
Melbourne, Victoria 3128
Australia
03.890.7947, Fax: 03.890.7947

Landini, Tim 21211 West Ten Mile Road, #507
Southfield, MI 48075

Larson, Jon 2339 10th Street
Berkeley, CA 94710
510.204.9346, Fax: 510.654.3424

Law, Candace 1864 Ellwood Avenue
Berkeley, MI 48072

Lee, Sun-Ho Suk Jun Building, #601
364.31 Seogko-Dong
Mapo-Ku, Seoul
Korea
02.334.2118x7090, Fax: 02.338.9416

Leffingwell, Les 12623 West Prospect Drive
New Berlin, WI 53151
414.782.4808

Library Canadian Centre for Architecture
1920 rue Baile
Montreal, QUE H3H 2S6
Canada
514.939.7000, Fax: 514.939.7020

Lichocki, Rose 1449 Lk. Nepessing Road
Lapeer, MI 48446

Linn, Laura Clayton HOK Illustration
211 North Broadway, Suite 600
St. Louis, MO 63102.2733
314.421.2000, Fax: 314.421.6073

Linton, Harold 37776 Turnberry Court
Farmington Hills, MI 48331

Lo, Julia 501 Elm, Suite 500
Dallas, TX 75202
214.748.2000, Fax: 214.761.0719

Lopez, Susan Architectonic Visualizations
50 Grant Drive
Avon, CT 06001
203.673.1992

Love, Edwin 815 Ridgeleigh Road
Baltimore, MD 21212
410.377.2969

Love, Ronald J. Ronald J. Love Architectural Illustration
3891 Bayridge Avenue
West Vancouver, BC V7V 3J3
Canada
604.922.3033, Fax: 604.922.2393

MacTavish, Cameron, AIA Voith & MacTavish
1616 Walnut Street
Philadelphia, PA 19103.5301
215.923.2222, Fax: 215.545.3299

Maggiore, Ray Archetype
138 West 19th Street, #1C
New York, NY 10011
516.621.4772

Magyar, Peter
Spaceprint, Inc.
632 Beaumont Drive
State College, PA 16801
814.466.3054, Fax: 814.865.3289

Mamiya, Sachiko
Takenaka Corporation
Kohee 1-B 11.1 Rokunotsubo-Cho
Matsugasaki Sakyo-ku, Kyoto 606
Japan
075.791.3536, Fax: 075.791.3536

Manus, Charles
Architectural Presentation Arts
43 Union Avenue, #1
Memphis, TN 38103
901.525.4335, Fax: 901.527.1143

Margolis, John
Margolis, Inc.
380 Boylston Street
Boston, MA 02116
508.470.3860

Maricak, Gretchen
1040 Chapin Street
Birmingham, MI 48009
810.542.3722

Martyniak, Philippe
13 Quai Du Commerce
Lyon 69009
France
33.78.64.83.59, Fax: 33.78.64.83.72

Matsuda, Yasuko
5.21.6, Katsutadai
Yachiyo, Chiba 276
Japan
0474.83.8574

Matuszczak, Jan
PO Box 145
Warrandyte, Vic 3113
Australia
613.844.2090, Fax: 613.844.1772

Maurice, Scott
21211 West Ten Mil Road, #515
Southfield, MI 48075

McBride, William A.
WAM Architectural Illustration
3518 Genessee, Suite 2
South, Kansas City, MO 64111.3918
816.756.0378, Fax: 816.756.0378

McCann, Michael
2 Gibson Avenue
Toronto, ONT M5R 1T5
Canada
416.964.7532, Fax: 416.964.2060

McIlhargey, Robert
1639 West 2nd Avenue, #410
Vancouver, BC V6J 1H3
Canada
604.736.7897, Fax: 604.736.9763

Meyers, Bruce
7421 Pebble Pointe
West Bloomfield, MI 48233

Miyamoto, Toshihiro
4.15.35 Takaai Higashi Sumiyoshiku
Osaka
Japan
06.697.1902, Fax: 06.697.1903

Mochizuki, Ayako
Takenaka Corporation
13.204 Nishiisya-danchi, 1.19 Kameooi
Meito-ku, Nagoya, Aichi 465
Japan
052.701.4235, Fax: 052.201.1252

Morello, Barbara
Morello Design Studio GMBH
Obere Donau Street 69/19
Vienna 1020
Austria
431.216.36.37, Fax: 431.216.36.37.15

Morris, Michael
5716 Crown
Westland, MI 48185

Morrissey, Michael
223 Indian Road Crescent
Toronto, ONT M6P 2G6
Canada
416.763.1387

Mullen, Richard
Presentation Art
203 West Holly Street, Suite 223
Bellingham, WA 98225
360.676.5352, Fax: 360.647.6056

Nakaoka, Akiko
Naito 1.2.7.2.153
Kokubunji, Tokyo 185
Japan
0425.77.3801, Fax: 0425.77.0616

Nastwold, Gail
24431 Bashian
Novi, MI 48075

Nelson, Mark
Nelson Design
3205 S. Maple Avenue
Berwyn, IL 60402.2809
708.484.3881

Nishikawa, Hideyo
Hainesukitahama 302, 1.4.1
hiranomati, chuo-ku
Osaka city, Osaka 541
Japan
06.202.2755, Fax: 06.202.2755

Nobles, David
Impulse Images & Animations, Inc.
9310 Autumn Sunrise
San Antonio, TX 78250
210.521.7221, Fax: 210.521.7343

Nodzykowski, Andrew
3152 Canfield Crescent
N. Vancouver, BC V7R 2V8
Canada
604.980.8339

Nojima, Michiko
F131 Kosumo Kameid Bunka 205
17.1 2-Chome Bunka
Sumida-Ku, Tokyo 131
Japan
03.3616.1287

O'Beirne, Michael
42 Eighth Street, #5213
Boston, MA 02129
617.241.8029

Ogasawara, Shigeru
3.6.10.301 Kouenji Minami
Suginamiku, Tokyo 166
Japan
03.3315.4569

Ogawa, Hiroshi
22.14.2F Maruymacho
Sibuya, Tokyo 150
Japan
03.3463.5968, Fax: 03.3770.4456

Ohira, Zensei
4.7.24.202 Hakusam
Bunkyo-ku, Tokyo 112
Japan
03.5978.4978, Fax: 03.5978.4978

Ohno, Hajime
Ozu-Atelier Inc.
2.2i6.11 Minami Aoyama
Tokyo 107
Japan
03.3408.4766, Fax: 03.3470.3159

Okumura, Kazuya
Human Factor, Ltd.
Wakamatsu Bld., 3.23.10 Sendagaya
Shibuya-ku, Tokyo 151
Japan
03.3402.2683, Fax: 03.3402.6629

Oles, Paul Stevenson, FAIA	Interface Architects One Gateway Center, Suite 501A Newton, MA 02158 617.527.6790, Fax: 617.527.6790
Oliver, Amy	67 Prall Street Pontiac, MI 48341
Onwukwe, Kay	4011 Maidstone Drive Gahanna, OH 43230 614.258.5553, Fax: 614.258.5578
Orest Associates	3757 Main Highway, PO Box 378 Miami, FL 33133 305.446.8159, Fax: 305.444.7709
Ortenberg, Alexander	PO Box 51343 Pacific Grove, CA 93950 408.384.7781
Ostergaard, Paul, AIA	UDA Architects 1133 Penn Avenue Pittsburgh, PA 15222 412.765.1133, Fax: 412.765.1902
Ozawa, Kaori	3.6.10.301 Kouenji Minami Suginamiku, Tokyo 166 Japan 03.3315.4569
Page, Wesley	233 North Blake Road Norfolk, VA 23505 804.627.5775, Fax: 804.622.1012
Paresi, James Jr.	888 West Knoll Drive West Hollywood, CA 90069 213.627.7373, Fax: 213.627.9815
Parker, Stephen	Hellmuth, Obata & Kassabaum 211 North Broadway, Suite 600 St Louis, MO 63102.2733 314.421.2000, Fax: 314.421.6073
Payne, Hilary	Alto Stratus PO Box 1266 Winchester Bay, OR 97467 503.271.7435, Fax: 503.271.7435
Pearson, Wilbur	6880 S.W. 98th Street Miami, FL 33156 305.667.9811
Peri, Michele	16484 Jessica Macomb, MI 48042
Phillips, Merike	B. Phillips/M. Phillips Arch. III 711 61st Street Kenosha, WI 53143 414.658.8464, Fax: 414.658.3464
Poitra, Ann	12212 West Layton Avenue Morrison, CO 80465 303.820.5200, Fax: 303.933.0866
Polhemus, Rick	21211 West Ten Mile Road, #515 Southfield, MI 48075
Query, W. R., Jr.	4212 Kelly Elliot Road Arlington, TX 76016 214.601.0201
Radvenis, Eugene	410.1639 West 2nd Avenue Vancouver, BC V6J 1H3 Canada 604.736.5430, Fax: 604.736.9763
Ratner, Barbara Worth, AIA	Architectural Illustration 828 Charles Allen Drive NE Atlanta, GA 30308 404.876.3943, Fax: 404.876.3943

Reardon, Michael	5433 Boyd Avenue Oakland, CA 94618 510.655.7030, Fax: 510.655.7030
Regan, Eamon	Sutton Sullenberger Yantis 1952 Gallows Road, Suite 100 Vienna, VA 22182 703.734.9733, Fax: 703.847.9171
Rice, Travis	3333 Grand Avenue, #244 Des Moines, IA 50312 515.274.4925, Fax: 505.274.6937
Rich, Stephen, AIA	85 Main Street Saugus, MA 01906 617.246.5200
Ringman, Samuel C.	Ringman Design and Illustration 1800 McKinney Avenue Dallas, TX 75201 214.871.9001, Fax: 214.871.3307
Rochon, Richard	13530 Michigan Avenue, Suite 205 Dearborn, MI 48126 313.584.9580, Fax: 313.584.4071
Rose, Ronald, Jr.,	Art Associates 4635 West Alexis Road Toledo, OH 43623 419.537.1303, Fax: 419.474.9113
Rosner, Joyce	The Rosner Studio 4916 Kelvin Street, #2 Houston, TX 77005 713.528.5446, Fax: 713.526.4088
Rossberg, Cheryl	21 North Kennicott Avenue Arlington Heights, IL 60005 708.925.6318
Rost, Steve	Lawrence Tech/Coll Arch & Design 21000 West Ten Mile Road Southfield, MI 48075
Rother, Christine	715 Bradford Alley Philadelphia, PA 19147 215.925.8449
Rusch, Al, AIA	Phillips Swager Associates 3622 North Knoxville Avenue Peoria, IL 61603
Rush, Richard	768 North Bucknell Street Philadelphia, PA 19130 215.763.8372
Saito, Ryuichi	Takenaka Corporation 21.1 8-Chome, Ginza Chuo-Ku, Tokyo 104 Japan 03.3542.7100, Fax: 03.3546.6765
Sakal, Ronald	Sakal and Hood, Architects 1012 Colley Avenue Norfolk, VA 23507 804.622.6991, Fax: 804.622.6991
Sampson, Philip	Leo A. Daly 8600 Indian Hills Drive Omaha, NE 68114 402.391.8111, Fax: 402.391.8564
Sanocki, Anne	21211 West Ten Mile Road, #615 Southfield, MI 48075
Schaller, Thomas Wells, AIA	Schaller Architectural Illustration 2112 Broadway, Suite 407 New York, NY 10023 212.362.5524, Fax: 212.362.5719

Schleef, Eric Eric Schleef Illustration
7740 Dean Road
Indianapolis, IN 46240
317.595.0016, Fax: 317.595.0016

Schmidt, Thomas 1020 Green Street, #104
Honolulu, HI 96822
808.524.5524

Schneider, George Watercolors by Schneider
804 South Fifth Street
Columbus, OH 43206
614.443.7014

Scholten, Robert 5036 Foxhill Drive
Longmont, CO 80501
303.772.8754, Fax: 303.772.8754

Scott, Jack 899 South Plymouth Court, #609
Chicago, IL 60605.2043
312.922.1467

Sedlock, Daniel 23705 Walden Court
Southfield, MI 48034

Shaw, Tracey Jane Grealy & Associates PTY LTD
7/322 Old Cleveland Road, Coorparoo
Brisbane, QLD 4151
Australia
617.394.4333, Fax: 617.849.0646

Sherrill, Thomas G. Caperton, Johnson, Inc.
14860 Montfort, Suite 200
Dallas, TX 75240
214.991.7082, Fax: 214.991.2578

Shilletto, George Young + Wright Architects Inc.
172 St. George Street
Toronto, ONT M5R 2M7
Canada
416.968.3522

Shimada, Kazuko 7.3.4.404 Hikarigaoka Nerima-ku
Nerima-ku, Tokyo 179
Japan
03.3939.8522, Fax: 03.3939.8522

Shimamoto, Lynn 6320 16th Avenue N.E.
Seattle, WA 98115
206.522.6851, Fax: 206.527.8680

Shirai, Hideo 31.8.213 Honcho
Wako-shi, Saitama-Ken 351.01
Japan
0484.65.1615, Fax: 048.465.1615

Shoda, Hisae Takenaka Corporation
8.24.305, 2-Chome Deguchi
Hirakata-shi, Osaka 573
Japan
0720.35.2690

Simontov, Slava 119 Aloha Street
Seattle, WA 98109
206.285.5267, Fax: 206.285.5267

Skordas, Yianni Skidmore Owings & Merrill
220 East 42nd Street
New York, NY 10017
212.309.9500

Slutsky, Rael D., AIA Rael D. Slutsky & Associates, Inc.
8 South Michigan Avenue, Suite 310
Chicago, IL 60603
312.580.1995, Fax: 312.580.1980

Smith, Clark 63 Fulton Street
Weehawken, NJ 07087
201.902.9656, Fax: 201.974.1645

Smith, James C. 700 South Clinton Street
Chicago, IL 60607
312.987.0132, Fax: 312.987.0099

Smith, Peter, AIA Campbell/Smith Architects
PO Box 1450
Duxbury, MA 02331
617.934.7181, Fax: 617.934.6488

Smith, Ryan 6855 Weddel
Taylor, MI 48180

Sneary, Richard Sneary Architectural Illustration
9728 Overhill Road
Kansas City, MO 64134
816.765.7841, Fax: 816.763.0848

Spira, Bill 53 Pleasant Road
Guelph, ONT N1E 3Z5
Canada

Stadler, Roger 21815 Purdue
Farmington Hills, MI 48336

Still, Irene 8 Victoria Street
Watsons Bay 2030
NSW, Australia
61.02.337.2801, Fax: 61.02.337.6146

Stracke, Charlene 4416 Charles Street
Dearborn, MI 48126

Sylvester, David Sylvester Illustration
441 Vannest Avenue
Trenton, NJ 08618
609.882.4360, Fax: 609.882.4360

Szasz, Peter 150 Green Street
San Francisco, CA 94111
415.982.3868, Fax: 415.781.3696

Szroborz, Stanislaw Atelier Szroborz
Merowingerstr. 120
Dusseldorf 40225
Germany
0211.317.96.93, Fax: 0211.317.95.92

Tainer, Dario AIA Tainer Assoiciates, LTD.
445 West Erie Street
Chicago, IL 60610
312.951.1656, Fax: 312.951.8773

Takahata, Masakazu Takenaka Corporation
1.38.21 Kuzuha Noda
Hirakata-shi, Osaka 573
Japan
0720.57.4044, Fax: 0720.57.4044

Tansantisuk, Mongkol, AIA 672 Grove Street
Newton Lower Falls, MA 02162
617.332.7885, Fax: 617.332.3789

Tchoban, Sergei NPS u. Partner
Ulmenstrasse 40
22299 Hamburg
Germany
49.40.48061848, Fax: 49.40.470027

Thibault, Rene 407.1509 Centre Street S.W.
Calgary, ALB T2G 2E6
Canada
403.262.4383, Fax: 403.265.4105

Tokita, Keiko 983.9 Kouwaen
Kuwana, Mie 511
Japan
0594.22.6460, Fax: 0594.21.8764

Tolon, Canan Tolon Design
814 Camelia Street
Berkeley, CA 94710
510.528.3007, Fax: 510.528.3009

Tsujimoto, Satohiro 1.3.14 Karasugatsuji Tennoji-ku
Osaka 543
Japan
06.779.9111, Fax: 06.779.9121

Tsurumaki, Akihide 19.14.201 2-Chome Kichijoji-Kitamachi
Musasino-shi, Tokyo 180
Japan
0422.201.77, Fax: 0422.20.1077

Ueland, Mark, AIA Ueland, Junker & McCauley Architects
718 Arch Street 5N
Philadelphia, PA 19106
215.440.0190, Fax: 215.440.0197

van den Hoed, Willem 1000 Huizen
Lange Geer 44, Delft 2611 PW
Holland
3115.133382, Fax: 3115.120448

Vangreen, Walter 81 Irving Place, #14A
New York, NY 10003.2217
212.420.0421

Visser, Evan 3050 Gold Dust NE
Belmont, MI 49306
616.676.0890

Vitullo, Richard James 342 Cedar Trail
Crownsville, MD 21032
410.923.1140

Wakita, Masanari Takenaka Corporation
1.26 Higashiyamamoto-machi Chikusa
Nagoya, Aichi 464
Japan
052.781.4474, Fax: 052.201.1252

Walker, Anthony 31433 Merriwood Park Drive
Livonia, MI 48152

Wang, Sung Ja Art Plan, Room 403, Saeleem Building
1158.5 Cholyang 3Dong Dong-Gu
Pusan, 601.013
Korea
051.462.9428, Fax: 051.465.2346

Watanabe, Koji 2.20.3, 2-Chome, Ibukino
Izumi-shi, Osaka 594
Japan
0725.56.7608, Fax: 0725.56.7608

Watanabe, Nao K,VC Inc.
Wakamathu Building, 3.23.10, Sendagaya
Shibuya-ku, Tokyo 151
Japan
3.3401.5877, Fax: 3.3402.7185

Watel, Robert, Jr. Bob Watel Inc.
202 Parkland Avenue
St. Louis, MO 63122
314.821.9285, Fax: 314.821.9285

Weaver, Ralph Ralph Weaver Delineator
RD 1, Box 141
McVeytown, PA 17051
717.899.6985, Fax: 717.899.6985

Wee, Andrew S.K. 453 Upper East Coast Road, #03.03
The Summit, Singapore,1646
Singapore
4423115/258866, Fax: 441.6515

White, Wendy 1639 West 2nd Avenue, #410
Vancouver, BC V6J 1H3
Canada
604.736.7897

Whitman, Peter 77 North Washington Street
Boston, MA 02114
617.227.2932, Fax: 617.227.8316

Willis, Daniel, AIA 1921 North Oak Lane
State College, PA 16803
814.867.5459, Fax: 814.865.3289

Wise, Steven 6 Deep Hollow Lane
Lancaster, PA 17603
717.390.4608, Fax: 717.293.4451

Witvoet, Brad 7265 Azalea
Grand Rapids, MI 49508

Wolf, Max 3040 Telegraph Avenue, #3
Berkeley, CA 94705
510.845.0736

Woodfield, Rebecca 25016 Independence Drive, #9104
Farmington Hills, MI 48335

Woodhouse, Curtis James 4141 Lybyer Avenue
Miami, FL 33133
305.663.8347

Worobec, Michael RTKL Associates Inc.
1250 Connecticut Avenue NW
Washington, DC 20036
202.833.4400

Xiong, George 60 Pavane Linkway, #1915
Don Mills, ONT M3C 2Y6
Canada
416.696.9906, Fax: 416.696.6711

Yamada, Kunio Lions Mansion
Kak-2.9 Kikusaka-cho Chik-ku
Nagoya, Aichi 464
Japan
052.751.3811, Fax: 052.752.1199

Yamamoto, Tamotsu 15 Sleeper Street
Boston, MA 02210
617.542.1021, Fax: 617.451.0271

Yanagida, Emiko Hara Bldg 4F, 3.13.1 Hizoo
Sibuya-ku, Tokyo 150
Japan
03.3400.0371, Fax: 03.3498.1623

Yao, Jia 55 South Kukui Street, #3110
Honolulu, HI 96813
808.536.0606, Fax: 808.536.0606

Yin, Jerry NBBJ
111 South Jackson Street
Seattle, WA 98104
206.223.5168, Fax: 206.621.2304

Yoshida, Fujio 301, 4.7.11, Zuiko, Higashiyodogawa-ku
Osaka-shi, Osaka 533
Japan
06.327.4947, Fax: 06.327.4947

Zaleski, Serge, ARAIA Delineation Graphix
238 Bulwara Road, Ultimo
Sydney, NSW 2007
Australia
61.2.552.3666, Fax: 61.2.692.9082

Zimmerman, Aaron 120 N.W. Parkway
Kansas City, MO 64150
816.587.9500, Fax: 816.587.1685

Zimmerman, Peter 5875 Cote St. Antoine
Montreal, QUE H4A 1S4
Canada
514.486.1331

Inquiries regarding membership in the Society, additional copies of AIP 10 or previous years' catalogues, orders for the hardcover title *Architecture In Perspective: A Five-Year Retrospective of Award-Winning Illustration*, or general information may be obtained by writing or phoning ASAP's executive director.

Officers

William G. Hook	President	206.622.3849
Tamotsu Yamamoto	Vice President	617.542.1021
Mongkol Tansantisuk, AIA	Treasurer	617.332.7885
Robert Becker	Secretary	914.591.5906
Paul Stevenson Oles, FAIA	Member at Large	617.527.6790

Advisory Council

Frank M. Costantino	617.846.4766
Elizabeth A. Day	512.469.6011
Gordon Grice, OAA, MRAIC	416.536.9191
Paul Stevenson Oles, FAIA	617.527.6790
Stephen W. Rich, AIA	617.224.6643
Thomas W. Schaller, AIA	212.362.5524
Rael Slutsky, AIA	312.580.1995
Dario Tainer, AIA	312.951.1656

Regional Coordinators

P.S. Oles, FAIA, Chairman	Boston, MA	617.527.6790
Stanley Doctor	Boulder, CO	303.449.3259
Richard Ferrier, FAIA	Arlington, TX	817.273.2801
Jeffrey M. George	San Francisco, CA	415.346.6621
Gordon Grice, OAA, MRAIC	Toronto, Ontario	416.536.9191
Dan Harmon	Atlanta, GA	404.609.9330
Sallie Hood	Norfolk, VA	804.622.6991
William G. Hook	Seattle, WA	206.622.3849
Michael McCann	Toronto, Ontario	416.964.7532
Richard Rochon	Dearborn, MI	313.584.958C
Thomas W. Schaller, AIA	New York, NY	212.362.552⁴
Thomas Schmidt	Honolulu, HI	808.524.5524
Rael Slutsky, AIA	Chicago, IL	312.580.199⁵
Robert G. Watel, Jr.	St. Louis, MO	314.821.9285

International Coordinators

Hans K. Chao	China	617.424.0205
Angelo DeCastro	Portugal	351.1.467.10 0
Miguelangel Gutierrez	Mexico	525.211.1921
Nobuo Kadowaki	Japan	3.3401.5877
Young Ki	Korea	708.843.3389
Hisao Konishi	Japan	81.75.802.2291
Sun-Ho Lee	Korea	02.334.2118x7C90
Phillipe Martyniak	France	33.78.6483.59
Sergei Tchoban	Germany	40.480618 48
Willem van Den Hoed	Holland	31.15.133382

Executive Director

Alexandra Lee	Boston	617.951.1433x225